POOLS PAR

A Farce in Three Acts

by

PHILIP KING

SAMUEL  FRENCH

LONDON
NEW YORK TORONTO SYDNEY HOLLYWOOD

ISBN 978-0-573-01349-2
www.samuelfrench.co.uk
www.samuelfrench.com

For Amateur Production Enquiries

United Kingdom and World
excluding North America
plays@samuelfrench.co.uk
020 7255 4302/01

Each title is subject to availability from Samuel French, depending upon country of performance.

POOLS PARADISE

Produced by Toby Rowland Ltd at the Phoenix Theatre, London, on the 16th February 1961, with the following cast of characters:

(in the order of their appearance)

Penelope Toop	*Pat Kirkwood*
Ida, the maid	*Vivian Pickles*
The Reverend Lionel Toop, Penelope's husband	*Hubert Gregg*
Miss Skillon	*Joan Sanderson*
Willie Briggs	*Patrick Blackwell*
The Reverend Arthur Humphrey	*Claude Hulbert*
The Bishop of Lax	*Henry Kendall*

Directed by Henry Kendall
Setting by Ken Calder

SYNOPSIS OF SCENES

The action of the Play passes in the lounge-hall of the Vicarage at the small village of Merton-cum-Middlewick

ACT I
A Saturday night in early December

ACT II
The following morning. 9.30 a.m.

ACT III
Fifteen minutes later

Time—the present

NOTE

Although the same setting is used, and all the characters are taken from it, this Play is *not* a sequel to *See How They Run.*

ACT I

SCENE—*The lounge-hall of the Vicarage at the small village of Merton-cum-Middlewick. A Saturday night in early December.*

It is a pleasantly furnished room with an arch down L *leading to the entrance hall. A staircase* L *runs up and off* L *to the bedrooms. A swing door under the stairs leads to the kitchen and back door. French windows up* RC *lead to a terrace and the garden. An open fireplace is* R *with the mantelpiece extending under the window above it. There are small windows* R *of the french windows, above the fireplace, down* R *and at the top of the stairs. A large built-in cupboard, with the door facing the audience, is in the corner between the french windows and the kitchen door up* L. *The cupboard has a small window in the wall* R. *Bookshelves are built into the side of the staircase. Down* R, *there is a desk and stool and below the desk is a small table with a pipe stand-cum-tobacco jar and a waste-paper basket. A tapestry fire-screen stands above the fireplace. There is a sofa* RC *with a small round table above the right end of it, on which there is a telephone. Upright chairs stand* L *of the french windows and against the bookshelves* L. *There is an armchair* LC *with a small table beside it. Between the foot of the stairs and the arch* L *there is a small sideboard with two mirrors and a religious plaque hanging on the wall over it. In the corner down* L *stands a carved armchair and a spinning-wheel. At night the room is lit by a five-branched chandelier* C, *a wall-bracket* L *and table-lamps on the desk and on the mantelpiece extension up* R. *These are controlled by switches above the arch* L *and at the top of the stairs. The cupboard has a practical light and switch. In the hall backing* L *there is an oval table with a wall-bracket light over it.*

When the CURTAIN *rises, the room is empty. All the lights are on, the window curtains are closed and the fire is lit. The telephone is ringing, not the "burr-burr", but long rings.* PENELOPE TOOP *enters at the top of the stairs, runs down, goes to the telephone and lifts the receiver.*

PENELOPE (*into the telephone*) The Vicarage, Merton-cum-Middlewick, Mrs Toop speaking . . . What name? . . . I'm sorry, I didn't quite catch . . . (*Patiently*) I'm sorry, but could you speak a little more distinctly? . . . (*With surprise*) You can't? But . . . (*Suddenly*) Oh, it's Mrs St John Soames. But you don't sound like her, somehow . . . You've dropped your what? . . . Ah, well, of course that explains it. I'm so sorry . . . The Vicar? . . . No, he's out at the moment, but could I give him a message? . . . (*She draws a pad and pencil towards her*) Just a moment, please, I'll write it down . . . Yes . . . (*She writes*) Mrs St John Soames has dropped and broken her upper set so will be unable to take Sunday School tomorrow . . . Thank you, Mrs St John Soames, he'll find someone to take your place . . . You're not to worry, you've got enough on your plate . . . I mean—well, good bye. (*She replaces the receiver, smiles to herself, moves to the front of the sofa, picks up a novel and lies on the sofa with her head at the left end*)

(*There is a slight pause as* PENELOPE *opens her book and starts to read.* IDA, *the maid, enters from the kitchen. She is a plain but likeable, almost whimsy village girl of eighteen. She is not in her uniform as it is her night out. Her going out apparel is gay but somewhat countrified. She carries her handbag. She does not see Penelope on the sofa. As soon as she gets into the room her eyes turn to all the lamps burning brightly*)

IDA. Oooh! All these lights. If Mr Toop was to see he'd go crackers. (*Eager to avoid trouble she dashes to the light switches above the arch down* L *and switches off all the lights, then turns and bumps into the armchair* LC)

(PENELOPE'S *voice is heard in the darkness*)

PENELOPE (*firmly but not nastily*) Ida, do you *mind!*

(IDA *gives a squeal of fright*)

IDA (*in the darkness*) Ow! Oh, my goodness! (*She pants*) Ow! (*She pants*) Is that you'm?

PENELOPE. It *is*.

IDA. I can't see'm.

PENELOPE. Neither can I. But I should like to.

IDA. Yes'm. Half a jiffy. (*She is heard stumbling towards the switch* L *where she switches on the chandelier*) There! (*She blinks in the light and looks around but still does not see Penelope*)

(PENELOPE *sits up suddenly and looks at Ida over the end of the sofa*)

PENELOPE. Hya!

IDA (*with a little start*) Ow! (*She moves below the armchair* LC) Oh, *there* you are! All by yourself in the dark.

PENELOPE. I wasn't in the dark until you . . .

IDA (*putting her bag on the table* LC *and crossing to* C) It was seeing all these lights on'm; everyone of 'em burning their insides out. And after the way Mr Toop read us the riot act about economizing—when he got the electricity bill—and then to come in here and find—(*she counts as she points to the lamps, the chandelier first*) one, two, three, four, five—six, seven . . .

PENELOPE (*smiling*) Nine.

IDA. Nine lamps burning! Oooh,'m! It would have been enough to make him forget he was a clergyman.

(PENELOPE *smiles, rises, moves to the fireplace and looks at the clock*)

PENELOPE. But what are you doing here at this time? I thought you'd gone out.

IDA (*moving to the table* LC) I'm waiting for that Willie Briggs'm. (*She takes her compact from her bag and opens it*) He's supposed to be calling for me. He's half an hour late already. (*She mutters as she shakes her powder-puff*) I'll "Willie Briggs" 'im. (*Annoyed*) We shall *miss* the serial. (*She dabs her nose*)

PENELOPE. I thought you were going into Badcaster, to the pictures?

Ida (*blinking at Penelope*) Pictures? Ooh! Aren't you old-fashioned? No'm—the telly. Mrs Muddle, next door to mum's got it, and she lets Willie and me go in to see the serial, 'cos, you see—(*she replaces her compact in her bag*) it's a *love story*, and after we've seen it, Willie and me go for our walk, and—well—it puts him in the mood, in a manner of speaking. It was like that last week, and Willie—when we went for our walk—well, honestly'm, I 'ad to give him a piece of my mind.

(Penelope *turns to the fireplace to hide her laughter*)

And it was all through the telly. (*Placidly*) You ought to have one up here in the Vicarage'm.

Penelope (*turning to Ida; with mock severity*) Ida, what do you mean?

Ida. Well, Mr Toop . . .

Penelope (*hastily*) That will do, Ida.

Ida. I was only going to say—Mr Toop's out such a lot, it'd be company for *you*'m.

Penelope. Oh! Oh, I see. (*She takes a cigarette from the box on the mantelpiece, and lights it*) We can't afford it.

Ida (*crossing to the chair* L) Well, no more can anybody else, but they '*ave* it. (*She picks up a book from the chair and puts it in the bookshelves*)

Penelope. I shouldn't like to put that argument to Mr Toop.

Ida. Oh, well, never mind. (*With a touch of mystery*) Wait till—(*she looks around her cautiously before continuing*) *our ship* comes home, then you can have a dozen tellys.

Penelope. Our—ship?

Ida (*quickly*) Sssh! You know what they say'm—"Even walls have ears".

(*The sound is heard of a car horn and of a car arriving and stopping*)

(*She listens*) There, you see? There's Mr Toop. Just shows how careful you have to be. Ow! (*She picks up her handbag and crosses to* L *of the sofa*) I'd forgotten what I'd come for, before I went.

Penelope. And what had you . . . ?

Ida (*apologetically*) The sixpence'm.

Penelope (*puzzled*) The sixpence?

Ida. Yes'm, for the—you know—what we were just talking about. (*She looks cautiously around*)

Penelope. Oh, yes, of course. (*She moves to the warming-pan hanging above the fireplace and takes out a sixpence from it*) Here you are, Ida.

(Ida *moves above the sofa, almost snatches the sixpence and hurriedly puts it in her handbag*)

Ida. Let's put it away quickly. We don't want Mr Toop asking awkward questions, do we'm?

Penelope (*laughing*) Really, Ida, I'm beginning to think you look upon my poor dear husband as—as a monster from outer space.

Ida (*almost indignantly*) Oh, no'm! Mr Toop's all right, really.

I'm sure he has one or two very good points. But, of course, being a clergyman, with his collar back to front—well, he's—handicapped from the start, isn't he? Don't know whether 'e's comin' or goin', do 'e?

(*The lights come on in the hall off* L)

PENELOPE (*waving a hand at Ida*) Go away—go away.
IDA (*moving to the kitchen door; happily*) Yes'm.
PENELOPE. Oh, just a minute.

(IDA *stops and turns*)

Did we remember the hot-water bottles tonight?
IDA (*trying to remember*) Oh—did we now? I wonder.
PENELOPE (*smiling*) Pop up and see, there's a dear. (*She looks towards the stairs*)
IDA. That's an idea'm. (*She goes up the stairs*) And if you hear the back-door bell'm, don't you answer it. It'll only be Willie Briggs, and it'll do *him* good to wait for a change.

(IDA *exits at the top of the stairs.* PENELOPE *smiles, moves below the sofa, lies on it as before, picks up her book and reads.*
The REVEREND LIONEL TOOP *enters down* L. *He is a man of thirty-six, of medium height, pleasant-faced, though of somewhat staid expression. He wears an overcoat over his black suit*)

LIONEL (*stopping; remembering*) Oh! (*He returns to the arch, switches off the hall light, then goes to the cupboard, opens the door, switches on the cupboard light, removes his hat, hangs it in the cupboard and closes the door. He opens the cupboard door, switches off the light, closes the door then moves to the stairs and goes up them. Very peeved*) Really! Five lights blazing and not a soul in the . . .

(LIONEL, *at the top of the stairs, switches off the chandelier and exits. The room is again in total darkness.* PENELOPE *is heard to close her book with a bang*)

PENELOPE (*in the darkness; with feeling*) Damn and blast! (*Unseen, of course, she jumps up and, really annoyed, begins to cross to the arch* L *to switch on the lights. Half-way across the room she stumbles over the table* LC, *which, together with the jar of tobacco, ashtray and magazines on it, clatters to the floor. She gives a cry of anguish*) Oh! My ankle! My foot! My leg! Ooh! (*She calls*) Help! Help! *Lights! Lights!* Help!

(LIONEL *enters in the darkness at the top of the stairs*)

LIONEL. What on earth . . . ? Penelope, is that you?
PENELOPE (*shouting*) *Lights!*

(LIONEL, *at the top of the stairs, switches on the chandelier.* PENELOPE *is on the floor,* C, *by the overturned table, clutching her ankle. Her eyes are closed in pain*)

LIONEL. Penelope! What are you doing on the floor? What's happened? (*He runs down the stairs*)

(IDA *enters at the top of the stairs*)

IDA (*alarmed*) What is it'm? What's . . . ?
PENELOPE (*her eyes still closed; calling louder than ever*) *Lights!*
IDA (*wildly*) Yes, 'm. (*She switches off the chandelier by the switch at the top of the stairs*)

(*The room is again plunged into darkness.* LIONEL, *half-way down the stairs, gives a terrified cry*)

PENELOPE (*opening her eyes*) *Lights!*
LIONEL (*shouting*) *Lights!*

(IDA *switches on the chandelier, and is seen with her hand on the switch, her eyes goggling.* LIONEL *is clinging to the banister half-way down the stairs.* PENELOPE *is still on the floor, rubbing her ankle*)

IDA (*gazing down on the scene*) Ow! What a to-do!
LIONEL (*gasping*) Oh, my—oh, my goodness!
IDA. Ooh, sir!
LIONEL (*anxiously*) Penelope, are you . . . ?
IDA (*brightly*) *I'll* see to Mrs Toop, sir. (*She runs down the stairs at a terrific speed*)
LIONEL (*as Ida approaches him; terrified*) Aah!

(IDA *pulls up very quickly just when it looks as if she must fall over Lionel*)

IDA (*when she has stopped; easily*) 'Scuse me. (*She squeezes past Lionel*)

(LIONEL *clings to the banister, expecting the worst*)

(*As she passes Lionel*) That's right, squeeze in a bit. (*She passes him*) There we are! (*She continues down the stairs*) Now, then . . .

(PENELOPE *gives a groan*)

Oh, poor Mrs Toop. (*She moves to Penelope*)
LIONEL (*moving down the stairs*) Ida, will you *please* . . .
IDA. In a minute, sir. One thing at a time. (*She crosses to Penelope*)

(PENELOPE *moans*)

(*She looks at the debris on the floor*) Oh, dear! What a mess! (*She picks up the tobacco jar. Suddenly*) And, oh—look! (*With great concern*) Look at your tobacco—all over the floor.
PENELOPE. Ida, for heaven's sake! Put that damned thing down and . . .

(IDA *gives the jar to Lionel*)

LIONEL. Penelope! There is no need for bad language.
PENELOPE (*grimly*) *Isn't* there? (*To Ida*) Get me on to the sofa before I begin throwing things. (*She squirms*) My ankle . . .

(IDA *helps* PENELOPE *to rise*)

IDA (*with great fuss*) There, now. Come along. Oops-a-daisy! *That's* better.

Penelope. It isn't! You're treading on my hand. Aah!

Ida (*calmly and soothingly*) Now, now! We must be brave, mustn't we? Remember, it hurts me just as much as it does you.

(Ida *helps* Penelope *to the sofa*)

Penelope. Ida! If you don't shut up I'll—I'll—clock you one.

Lionel (*horrified*) Really! Such lack of control.

(Penelope *stops, turns, and pulls an evil face at Lionel, showing her teeth*)

Penelope. Grrrh! (*She limps below the sofa*)

Lionel (*anxiously*) There's nothing broken, is there?

Penelope. Every bone that isn't broken's bent. (*She sits* c *of the sofa*)

Lionel. It could have been worse. (*He glances at Ida*) Much worse I might have broken my neck. (*He stands the table on its feet and puts the tobacco jar on it*)

Ida (*innocently*) You're lucky, aren't you, sir? But they do say, "The devil looks after his own." (*She picks up the ashtray, magazines, etc., and puts them on the table*)

Lionel. Ida, will you please keep quiet. (*He turns to face her*) If you hadn't stupidly plunged the room into darkness I should never have . . .

Penelope (*snapping at Lionel*) And if you hadn't done the same silly trick *I* shouldn't have, either.

(Ida *looks at the magazines*)

Lionel (*crossing to* l *of the sofa*) Penelope, please! Er—*prenez garde —la domestique.*

Penelope. *Prenez garde* yourself!

Lionel. Is your ankle giving you much pain?

Penelope (*shortly*) It's giving me hell!

(Lionel *gulps but refrains from comment.* Ida *is engrossed in the magazine*)

Lionel. Do you think we should get the doctor? Or the district nurse? (*With a sudden thought*) Or I *could* ring Miss Skillon.

Penelope (*aghast*) *What?*

Lionel. Miss Skillon *is* a member of the St John Ambulance Brigade.

Penelope (*firmly*) If you bring that woman near me I'll—I'll bite lumps out of her. Ida, I don't wish to disturb you——

(Ida *puts the magazine on the table* lc *and crosses to* l *of Lionel*)

—but would you get a handkerchief, soak it in cold water, *squeeze* it out and bring it here. Not one of mine, one of Mr Toop's.

Ida. Yes'm. Excuse me, sir. (*She takes the handkerchief from Lionel's breast pocket*)

Penelope. Pronto!

Ida. Yes'm.

(Ida *exits up the stairs*)

Lionel (*pained*) Penelope, must you? "Pronto"! (*With a sigh*) Oh, dear, dear, dear! Your theatrical career has left you with a very lamentable legacy.

Penelope. Lionel, I am in no mood to listen to ecclesiastical pomposity. (*Before he can reply*) And you might have the decency to say how sorry you are. You realize—(*she points to her ankle*) this is your fault, don't you?

Lionel. Frankly—no.

Penelope. If you hadn't turned the lights out in here . . .

Lionel (*firmly*) Five lights burning and not a soul in the room.

Penelope (*almost wildly*) For heaven's sake, man! I was in the room.

Lionel (*firmly*) Not when I came in.

Penelope (*muttering*) Give me strength! (*As if explaining to a child*) I was *here*—on the sofa—*reading*.

Lionel. Oh! (*Rather frigidly*) Oh, then in that case, I apologize. But I still don't see why it was necessary to have five lights burning. One lamp—(*he indicates the table-lamp up* R) would have been quite sufficient.

Penelope. You know, Lionel, you really are very two-faced.

Lionel. Two-faced?

(Penelope *discreetly unfastens her stocking from its suspender*)

Penelope. Yes. Every Sunday in church it's "Lighten our Darkness" and the moment you get home it's—darken our lightness.

Lionel. I told you yesterday and I can only repeat—our electricity bill is outrageous. I am not made of money. And I've just got to save up for the vicarage repairs.

Penelope (*vaguely*) Yes, darling. Pull my stocking off, will you?

Lionel. Er—what?

Penelope (*slightly exasperated*) I can't manage it myself and I've got to get it off for the bandage.

Lionel. Oh—er—(*he looks apprehensively towards the stairs*) yes—well . . . (*He moves to Penelope*)

Penelope. Lionel, *dar*ling! I'm only asking you to pull my stocking off. It's only nine o'clock.

Lionel (*about to expostulate*) I—I . . . (*He motions her to lift her skirt, takes off her shoe and pulls off her stocking*) Penelope, I don't believe you take me seriously.

Penelope. Darling, the day I do, I shall either apply for a divorce or go stark raving mad.

Lionel (*somewhat priggishly*) Will you please not make—abysmal quips after every remark I address to you. When I say you don't take me seriously I am referring to this matter of waste. (*He circles the sofa and moves down* LC) There is a need for economy in every direction. Take my church—every bell in my belfry is cracked—(*he moves and stands over Penelope, her stocking hanging down from his hand*) and as far as this house is concerned—at the rate we're going I shall soon be in the Bankruptcy Court. (*He moves around* C, *unconsciously swinging the stocking*) Heaven knows, I am not a mean man, am I? (*He waits for a second then turns and looks enquiringly at Penelope*) What did you say?

PENELOPE. Nothing.

LIONEL. Oh. Until recently I have always found my stipend—er adequate. (*Grandly*) I don't ask for the earth. I don't ask for wealth.

PENELOPE (*quietly*) D'you know anyone to ask?

(LIONEL *ignores the remark and circles the armchair to* C)

LIONEL. And I am happy in the knowledge that every penny that comes into this house does so by the sweat of my own brow.

PENELOPE (*flippantly*) Oh, well, that's marvellous, isn't it? You're happy and—er—perspiring, so—you're all right, Jack!

LIONEL. Jack?

(IDA *enters at the top of the stairs carrying the now damp handkerchief*)

PENELOPE (*to Ida; not nastily*) Oh, Ida! I thought you'd gone to bed.

IDA (*happily*) Oh, no'm. Not on my night out. (*She comes down the stairs. As she is about to cross to Penelope she notices the stocking swinging from Lionel's hand, stops and gives a little giggle*)

(LIONEL *looks blankly at* IDA *who looks at him and giggles again. He looks at her more blankly.* IDA, *with one finger, points to the stocking and giggles.* LIONEL, *realizing at last what Ida is giggling at, confusedly crumples the stocking and puts it in his breast pocket*)

(*She gives another giggle and crosses to Penelope*) Well, now! Shall I be nurse'm? (*Happily*) You can be matron, sir. (*She sits* L *of Penelope on the sofa and begins to wind the handkerchief around Penelope's leg, just below the knee*)

PENELOPE (*patiently*) Ida, my ankle is slightly lower down—or it was ten minutes ago.

IDA (*with a laugh*) Oh, of course. (*To Lionel*) Aren't I a silly? (*She looks happily towards Lionel*)

(LIONEL *glares frigidly at Ida*)

(*She sobers up and hastily bandages Penelope's ankle*) I'm not hurting you, am I, m'm?

PENELOPE (*wincing*) No, no! I am enjoying it immensely.

LIONEL (*moving above the sofa; frigidly*) If I might interrupt your enjoyment for a moment, Penelope. While we are on the subject of extravagance . . .

PENELOPE. I was rather hoping we were *off* it.

LIONEL (*inexorably*) Your house-keeping book.

PENELOPE. Oh, dear!

LIONEL. Where is it? It's quite a while since I saw it. I have half an hour to spare, so . . .

PENELOPE (*muttering*) You're a glutton for punishment. (*Brightly*) It's in the desk there. (*She points*) Help yourself.

LIONEL (*moving to the desk*) Thank you, I will.
PENELOPE. It's in the left-hand corner.

(LIONEL *looks in the pigeon-holes of the desk and takes out a slim book, a copy of "Lady Chatterley's Lover"*)

LIONEL (*blinking at the title*) Penelope, what is this book doing in the Vicarage?
PENELOPE (*smoothly*) Well, the Bishop of Woolwich said it was all right.

(LIONEL *replaces the book in the desk and takes out a very battered exercise-book*)

LIONEL. Ah! This looks more like it.
PENELOPE. Be careful, darling. I keep the housekeeping money in it. There may be the odd ten-shilling note.

(LIONEL *holds the bound edge of the book between his finger and thumb, holds it downward and shakes it. Nothing drops out*)

LIONEL (*coldly*) There is *no* ten-shilling note—odd or otherwise. (*He sits on the stool by the desk and turns over the pages*)
IDA (*finishing the bandaging*) 'Ow's that'm?
PENELOPE. Very pretty. I shall never walk again, but—thank you, Ida.
LIONEL (*looking at the book*) November, December. (*He rises*) I shall be in my den if I'm wanted. (*He crosses towards the stairs*) This housekeeping book of yours should make fascinating reading.
PENELOPE. It'd open up a whole new world to Selwyn Lloyd.
LIONEL (*ignoring this*) You going out, Ida? (*He stands above the table* LC)
IDA (*dropping Penelope's leg and rising*) Yes, sir. (*She moves to* L *of the sofa*)
LIONEL (*putting the exercise-book on the table* LC) Are you seeing Willie Briggs?
IDA. That was the idea. (*She giggles*)
LIONEL. Will you tell Willie I am very displeased with him.
IDA. Oh, sir!
LIONEL. Very displeased. He failed to appear at choir practice last night.
IDA (*explaining*) Oh, yes. But he *meant* to appear.
LIONEL. Magnanimous of him. But he didn't.
IDA. No. You see, he'd forgotten to post his—his . . . (*She falters*)
LIONEL. His what?
IDA (*glibly*) That's right. And he had to go back to the farm for it, and by the time he'd got back and been to the post, well—there didn't seem much point . . .
LIONEL. There doesn't seem much point in his being in the choir if he cannot attend practices. He knew very well we were having an extra rehearsal for the carol service. (*He moves to the stairs*) I was not at all happy about it last year.
PENELOPE. Nor was anybody else.

LIONEL (*rather stiffly*) Oh? I was not aware that any of the congregation had complained.
PENELOPE. All I'm saying is they didn't look happy. And you must admit, Lionel, that, on the whole, it *was* a bit of a shambles.
LIONEL (*moving below the armchair*) The carol service? A *shambles?*
PENELOPE. Well, *darling*—when *you* announce *God Rest Ye Merry Gentlemen* and the *organ* plays *There's No Business Like Show Business* . . .
LIONEL (*annoyed*) I will not stay and listen to such nonsense. (*He moves to the stairs. To Ida*) When you have put the room straight, you can bring a cup of coffee to me in the den.
IDA (*quickly*) Yes, sir. (*She darts to the kitchen door*) I'll go and pop it on the stove now.

(IDA *exits quickly to the kitchen*)

LIONEL (*trying to stop her*) There is no need to . . . I said, when you've . . .

(*But Ida has gone*)

Really, Penelope, that girl is quite impossible. It baffles me why we keep her. (*He starts up the stairs*)
PENELOPE (*somewhat roused*) It would baffle me still more to find anyone who would do *half* the work Ida does for twice the money.
LIONEL (*stopping half-way up the stairs; grudgingly*) I'm not saying she isn't a good worker.
PENELOPE. You certainly aren't; not in front of me. Ida is an absolute angel. She must be to put up with—us.
LIONEL (*coming down the stairs*) By "us" I presume you mean *me*. (*He stands above the armchair*)
PENELOPE. Well, darling—you do rather chivvy the girl, don't you?
LIONEL (*protesting*) *I*—chivvy . . . ?
PENELOPE. Just now, for instance. "Bring a cup of coffee to me in the den."
LIONEL (*baffled*) Well—a perfectly simple request.
PENELOPE (*patiently*) Lionel—this is Ida's *night out*. She should have gone half an hour ago.
LIONEL. Then why didn't she?
PENELOPE. She's waiting for Willie Briggs to call for her.
LIONEL. Waiting in the kitchen, I suppose?
PENELOPE. Yes.
LIONEL. Burning *my* electric light.
PENELOPE. Oh, *really*, darling!
LIONEL (*moving to* L *of the sofa*) The electricity bill I received yesterday . . .
PENELOPE. Lionel, if you mention that damned electricity bill again . . . We had it for breakfast, lunch and supper yesterday; breakfast and lunch today . . .
LIONEL (*circling the sofa to* C) And yet—*and yet*—I come into this room and find—(*he counts*) one, two, three . . .
PENELOPE. Five, five!

LIONEL. Ja! Ja! Er—five lamps burning.

PENELOPE. All right. All right. I accept full responsibility; I'm to blame, and I'm sorry, and it won't happen again, and instead of buying me a Christmas present use the money to help pay the electricity bill and for heaven's sake is there anything more I can do?

LIONEL. You can take a breath for one thing. (*Stiffly*) You can most certainly stop acting the martyr. (*He moves to the armchair and sits*) You know perfectly well I wouldn't dream of not buying you a Christmas present. (*He takes out his pipe*) Though—(*with a look towards the kitchen door*) unless that girl mends her ways, she will most certainly get nothing from *me* this year.

PENELOPE (*with a smile*) After what you gave her last year, I don't think that will worry Ida.

LIONEL (*protesting*) I gave her . . .

PENELOPE. I know, darling—a lovely book. *Pilgrim's Progress.*

LIONEL. I also slipped a five-shilling postal order between the pages.

PENELOPE. Well, if you slipped it anywhere beyond page three, she'd never have got it.

(LIONEL *rises, collects some spilled tobacco from the floor and puts it in his pipe*)

LIONEL. Incidentally—have you put in your Christmas orders with the shops yet?

PENELOPE. Not yet.

LIONEL. Before you do I think it would be as well if I were to look them over.

PENELOPE (*with a sigh*) Very well, Lionel.

LIONEL. And by the way—were you thinking of a turkey this year?

PENELOPE. If I *was*, it would be *very* by the way. (*With much reflection*) No, no—I believe Mr Jupp makes some very excellent beef sausages. And if we *could* run to a bottle of H.P. sauce . . .

LIONEL (*moving to* L *of the sofa*) Penelope, there is no need to be facetious. As a matter of fact, I should *like* you to get a turkey.

PENELOPE. You *would?*

LIONEL (*crossing to the fireplace*) Er—yes, my dear. (*He picks up a box of matches from the mantelpiece*)

PENELOPE. What about the electric light bill—why buy a turkey and eat it in the dark? And after all, there's only the two of us. I'm sure a couple of day-old chicks . . .

(LIONEL *ignores Penelope's last remark and lights his pipe*)

LIONEL (*somewhat uneasily*) I—I—I—rather thought we might invite—er—someone to spend Christmas Day with us.

PENELOPE. Oh. Who?

LIONEL. Someone who would otherwise spend it alone.

PENELOPE (*very suspiciously*) Just *who* is this someone?

LIONEL. Er—Miss—Miss . . .

PENELOPE (*quickly*) Not Miss *Skillon?*

Lionel. Precisely.

Penelope (*almost bursting*) *Lionel!*

Lionel (*quickly*) Penelope, I know exactly how you feel about Miss Skillon . . .

Penelope. And you also know how she feels about me.

Lionel. That's exactly how I feel about her.

Penelope. And yet you have the nerve to suggest she comes here for Christmas Day! That interfering busybody—that sex-starved . . .

Lionel (*with restraint*) "Lonely" is the word. Miss Skillon is one of my most ardent church workers, to boot.

Penelope. "To boot" is right, and she hates my guts.

Lionel. Penelope!

Penelope. And the way she looks at me. Just because I used to be on the stage. Anyone would think I'd been on the streets.

Lionel (*trying to speak patiently*) I am quite sure you and Miss Skillon would understand each other so much better if you could only get together over . . .

Penelope (*it is almost a yell*) Over a *turkey?* (*Firmly*) Not even over a *boiling* fowl.

(Lionel *crosses to the stairs, picking up the exercise-book as he passes the table* lc)

(*She sits up*) Lionel! You haven't actually invited her, have you?

Lionel. As a matter of fact, I *have.*

Penelope. And she accepted?

Lionel. She did.

Penelope (*leaping up to go to him*) Lionel! You—you . . . (*She gives a cry of pain and clutches her ankle*) *Ow!* (*She sits on the sofa and whimpers*) I'll never forgive you—never.

(Ida *enters from the kitchen carrying a tray with a cup of coffee and a bowl of sugar. The saucer is resting on the top of the cup*)

Ida (*brightly*) Here we are, sir. Here's your coffee. Shall I take it up to the den?

Lionel. No, thank you. Give it to me. (*He takes the saucer*) I don't want the tray, thank you.

(Ida *picks up the cup and sips from it*)

Ida. I 'aven't sugared it. How many?

Lionel. Three, if it's all right with you.

Ida (*not saucily*) 'Aven't 'alf got a sweet tooth, 'asn't 'e, mum? (*She puts three lumps of sugar into the cup and then hands the sugar bowl to Lionel*)

Lionel (*wearily*) Not as sweet as all that.

Ida. Oh, aren't I a silly? (*She takes the bowl and gives Lionel the cup*)

Lionel. Thank you. (*He goes up the stairs, turns, takes a drink from the cup and winces*) What *is* this—coffee or Oxo?

Ida (*quite seriously*) Coffee. I mean it *must* be; we've put *sugar* in it.

(LIONEL *is about to speak, thinks better of it, turns and stumps off at the top of the stairs.* PENELOPE *puts on her shoe, rises and hops to the radio up* R)

(*She puts the tray and bowl on the table* LC) Fancy him not knowing the difference. You all right'm?

PENELOPE. I am better in health than temper.

(*The front-door bell rings off* L)

IDA. Ow! Now whoever's that?

PENELOPE. Won't it be Willie Briggs?

IDA. What? At the front door. He'll hear my tongue if it is.

(IDA *switches on the hall light and exits down* L. PENELOPE *switches on the radio. There is a slight pause then the* ANNOUNCER'S *voice is heard*)

ANNOUNCER (*through the radio*) Good evening. In two minutes' time you will be hearing the second of four talks by Professor Zimmerman on the habits of the Himalayan anteater.

PENELOPE (*to herself*) That's all I need. (*She switches the radio off*)

(IDA *enters quickly down* L *and crosses below the armchair*)

IDA (*as she enters*) Please'm . . .

PENELOPE. Ida, I'm on the Third Programme. How do I get off it?

IDA (*excitedly*) You just twiddle'm. Please'm, it's Miss Skillon.

PENELOPE. What is?

IDA. It's Miss Skillon at the door.

PENELOPE. What does she want?

IDA. She's fiddle-diddling with her bicycle lamp. (*She laughs*) She says it's gone out and won't come on again. P'raps she's run out of oil.

PENELOPE. Foolish virgin! But what does she expect me to . . . ?

IDA. Oh, it isn't you she wants'm. It seems she's fiddle-diddled all she can, and she wonders if the Vicar would come and fiddle-diddle with her. (*She points off* L) She's on the doorstep.

PENELOPE. Push her off it.

IDA. 'Course it's all an excuse to see the Vicar; we know that, don't we'm?

PENELOPE. We certainly do.

IDA. Well, I'll say this for her, she never gives up.

PENELOPE. Well, get rid of her, Ida, for heaven's sake.

IDA. Yes'm, but 'ow?

PENELOPE. I don't care how. Tell her we're all in quarantine for distemper.

IDA. Yes'm. (*Happily*) Wouldn't it be funny if we were?

(IDA *exits down* L. PENELOPE *looks blankly after Ida then switches on the radio which bursts into "The Ride of the Valkyries" at top volume.* PENELOPE *recoils.*

IDA *bursts in down* L)

(*As she enters*) Please'm, *she's 'ere!*

(Penelope, *with her hand on the knob, turns quickly and automatically turns the knob, increasing the volume still further*)

Penelope. *What?*

(Miss Skillon *sweeps in down* L. *She is a large, rather sour spinster of thirty-five. She carries a handbag*)

Miss Skillon (*as she enters*) I hope I'm not a nuisance—(*she stops abruptly* L *of the armchair and claps her hands to her ears*) Aaaaah!

(Penelope, *agitated, turns the knob still higher*)

Penelope (*shouting*) So sorry, Miss Skillon.
Miss Skillon (*shouting*) Mrs Toop, really . . .

(Penelope *runs to Miss Skillon and shouts in her ear*)

Penelope. Sorry! Can't hear a word. (*She moves to the radio*) Ida! Come and help.
Ida (*crossing below Miss Skillon and nudging her as she passes*) Isn't she a caution?
Penelope (*frantically*) It'll blow up in a minute.
Ida. Hit it'm! Hit it!

(Penelope *hits the side of the radio with the flat of her hand and the music stops abruptly*)

Now turn it off, 'm, before it gets its second wind.

(Penelope *switches off the radio*)

Penelope. Bless you, Ida.

(Ida *collects the tray and sugar bowl and exits to the kitchen*)

Miss Skillon (*frigidly*) Mrs Toop—if you *could* spare me a moment of your time.
Penelope (*moving below the sofa*) Miss Skillon, I'm so sorry. And I do apologize for your somewhat unusual reception.
Miss Skillon (*frigidly*) Please don't apologize, Mrs Toop. We have long ceased to expect anything but the—er—unusual from you.
Penelope (*bristling*) Now, Miss Skillon . . .
Miss Skillon (*continuing quickly; with a thin smile*) That is what makes a visit to the Vicarage so—er—exciting.

(Penelope *gulps*)

Penelope (*indicating the sofa*) Won't you sit down and tell me what I can do for you?
Miss Skillon (*sitting in the armchair*) Thank you, Mrs Toop, I didn't mean to disturb *you*.
Penelope (*sweetly*) Of course you didn't. (*She sits on the sofa*)
Miss Skillon. It was the Vicar I wanted to—er . . .
Penelope. Disturb—quite.

(MISS SKILLON *glares.*
IDA *enters from the kitchen*)

(*To Ida; quickly; ignoring Miss Skillon's glare*) Ida, will you let the Vicar know Miss Skillon is here?

IDA. Yes'm. (*She darts up the stairs*) Lovely evenin', Miss Skillon.

PENELOPE. Well, now! I hear you've got yourself into trouble.

(IDA, *half-way up the stairs, reacts*)

MISS SKILLON (*sharply*) I beg your pardon?

(IDA *exits at the top of the stairs*)

PENELOPE (*with a smile*) Ida tells me your bicycle lamp is playing you up.

MISS SKILLON (*frigidly*) My bicycle lamp has gone out.

PENELOPE. Oil shortage?

MISS SKILLON. My bicycle lamp works from a battery.

PENELOPE (*sweetly*) That must be very nice.

MISS SKILLON. Mrs Toop . . .

PENELOPE. Except when it goes out.

(IDA *enters down the stairs*)

IDA. Mr Toop's just comin'm.

PENELOPE. Thank you, Ida.

(IDA *beams at Penelope then looks at Miss Skillon*)

IDA (*somewhat coldly*) 'Case I don't see you again, Miss Skillon, I'll say toodle-oo.

MISS SKILLON (*sourly*) Toodle-oo—er—good night.

IDA. Don't mention it.

(IDA *exits to the kitchen. There is a slight awkward pause*)

PENELOPE. It's—er—Ida's night out.

MISS SKILLON (*frigidly*) Really.

PENELOPE. Yes. (*She pauses*) She's waiting for Willie Briggs to call for her. (*She pauses*) He's her boy friend. (*She pauses*) Rather romantic, don't you think?

MISS SKILLON (*coldly*) Mrs Toop, I'm afraid I cannot arouse any interest in the romantic affairs of your domestic help.

PENELOPE. Oh. (*She pauses*) Well, that's a help, isn't it?

(LIONEL *enters at the top of the stairs*)

LIONEL (*descending the stairs*) Miss Skillon! I didn't expect—that is—er—this *is* a most unwanted pleasure—er—un*wonted*. I hope Penelope has been looking after you. Can we get you some coffee?

MISS SKILLON. No, thank you, Vicar.

PENELOPE (*quietly*) Or Oxo?

(LIONEL *and* MISS SKILLON *react*)

MISS SKILLON (*frigidly*) This is not a social call, Mrs Toop. (*To*

Lionel. With a complete change of tone) I wanted to see you, Vicar

LIONEL (*with an apprehensive glance at Penelope*) Oh—er—quite.

PENELOPE (*rising*) I'll leave you two alone . . .

LIONEL (*moving to* L *of the sofa; flustered*) No, no, Penelope. I'm sure there is no need to . . . (*With asperity*) Please sit down again. If your ankle really is sprained you shouldn't be—er—capering about on it.

PENELOPE (*sitting on the sofa; pleasantly*) I had no intention of "capering about", darling. I was merely going to retire and give Miss Skillon a chance to get whatever's *on* her chest *off* it. (*She smiles*) Within reason, of course.

LIONEL (*moving to* R *of Miss Skillon*) Er—have you got something on your chest, Miss Skillon?

MISS SKILLON. I have just come from the Institute, Vicar. I—er—happened to be passing, so thought I would look in.

LIONEL. How thoughtful. Were there many young people there?

MISS SKILLON. At least twenty—boys *and* girls.

LIONEL (*beaming*) Good! *Gooood!*

MISS SKILLON (*frigidly*) I doubt if you will think so when I tell you what they were doing.

PENELOPE (*murmuring*) I'm *so* glad I stayed.

LIONEL (*sharply*) Penelope! (*To Miss Skillon*) Er—what were they —er—doing, Miss Skillon?

MISS SKILLON. They were gambling.

LIONEL. *What?*

MISS SKILLON. With my own eyes I saw them.

LIONEL (*horrified*) Gambling in the Church Institute!

MISS SKILLON. I saw money on the table.

LIONEL (*really angry*) When I have expressly forbidden—when only last Sunday in my sermon I . . . (*He cannot go on*)

PENELOPE (*interested*) What were they playing, Miss Skillon? Pontoon?

MISS SKILLON (*frigidly*) Pon——?

PENELOPE (*glibly*) —toon. You know.

MISS SKILLON. No, Mrs Toop, I do *not* know.

PENELOPE (*fairly quickly*) Well, someone holds the bank; he deals a card all round, and the idea is to get twenty-one. You buy your other cards, of course. The ace is either high or low—eleven or one, whichever you wish, see?

LIONEL (*horrified*) Penelope!

(PENELOPE *becomes aware of the frozen stares of the other two*)

PENELOPE (*meekly*) I—I—used to watch the boys play it on train calls—when I was on tour. They would indulge sometimes—after they'd tired of Snakes and Ladders.

LIONEL. I will not have you treat gambling with levity. You know how I disapprove of it—in any shape or form.

PENELOPE. Yes, Lionel.

LIONEL. And I am determined to do all in my power to stamp it out here, in my parish.

MISS SKILLON. Well said, Vicar.

LIONEL. Thank you, Miss Skillon. (*Ponderously*) When Adam fell, it was decreed that, henceforth, Man should earn by the sweat of his brow, and not make easy money by cards—horse-racing—dog-racing, nor even Premium Bonds.

PENELOPE. And, darling, what's wrong with Premium Bonds?

LIONEL (*inexorably*) They are a form of gambling, and as such I disapprove of them.

MISS SKILLON. Well said, Vicar.

LIONEL. Thank you, Miss Skillon. There are none in this house, nor will there ever be.

PENELOPE (*dismayed*) Oh, Lord!

LIONEL. I beg your pardon? (*With a start*) Penelope, you *haven't . . . ?*

PENELOPE. 'Fraid so, dear.

LIONEL. *What?*

PENELOPE. I'm getting half a dozen as a Christmas present from uncle. (*To Miss Skillon*) My Uncle Dudley—the Bishop of Lax.

LIONEL (*gaping*) The Bishop sending you Premium Bonds?

PENELOPE. He is—bless him.

LIONEL (*helplessly*) I—I—I . . .

PENELOPE (*murmuring quietly*) Well said, Vicar.

LIONEL (*to Miss Skillon*) Miss Skillon—these—er—gamblers in the Institute—did you remonstrate with them?

MISS SKILLON. I tried to, Vicar. It was not easy. Really! The boys and girls of today!

LIONEL. Did you tell them you would inform me?

MISS SKILLON. I most certainly did.

LIONEL. Ah! And what did they say to that?

MISS SKILLON. I would rather not repeat it. Then, when I left the Institute I found my bicycle lamp out, and it would not come on again. I strongly suspect that the bulb had been interfered with.

LIONEL. I shall go across to the Institute at once. (*He goes to the cupboard, opens the door, switches on the light, gets his hat and scarf, switches out the light and closes the door*) These youngsters must be taught a lesson. It is my duty to make it clear to them that they can neither gamble in the Church Institute, *nor* interfere with Miss Skillon's bulbs.

(*The kitchen door is flung open and hits Lionel.*
IDA, *wild-eyed and gasping, enters from the kitchen*)

PENELOPE. Ida!

LIONEL (*very annoyed*) Ida, really! We cannot have you bursting into the room in this unseemly . . . What do you want?

IDA (*excitedly*) I want to go upstairs.

LIONEL. *What?*

IDA (*excitedly but innocently*) No, no, I don't mean for that, but . . . 'Scuse me. (*She rushes to the stairs*) It's in my bedroom. (*She starts up the stairs then stops and turns*) I've got to get it. (*She goes up another step or two then stops and turns*) Willie says it's no use without it, 'Scuse me.

(Ida *stumbles off at the top of the stairs*)

Lionel (*putting on his scarf; firmly*) Penelope, I warn you; unless you can exercise some control over that girl she will have to go. (*He puts his hat on the table* LC) Really! Bursting into the room like that.

Penelope. Darling, be fair. It's her night off. She's going out with her boy friend.

Lionel. That may be, but . . .

Penelope. I used to be just as excited when I was going out with you.

Lionel. There is no need to . . .

(Ida *enters breathlessly down the stairs*)

Ida (*as she descends; excitedly*) I've got it! (*She holds out a clenched hand*) I've got it! Wouldn't it've been awful if I'd lost it! 'Scuse me. (*She moves to* L *of Lionel*) I've got to get back to Willie, or he'll be running round the kitchen like a rampaging lion. You goin' out, sir? (*With a look towards Miss Skillon*) Thought you might be, some'ow. (*To Miss Skillon. Breathlessly and quickly*) 'Case I don't see you again, Miss Skillon, I'll say good night.

(Ida *darts off to the kitchen*)

Lionel (*pacing* C; *fuming*) Penelope!

Penelope. Darling, there isn't a single stamp on her cards, otherwise she'd leave first thing tomorrow morning.

(Lionel *takes the stocking from his pocket and mops his brow with it.* Miss Skillon *reacts.* Lionel *hastily pockets the stocking*)

Lionel (*testily*) I must get across to the Institute. (*He crosses to the arch* L) We will discuss that girl's future when I return.

Penelope. *If* you return.

Lionel. What?

Penelope. Well, you know what youngsters are like these days. They're apt to get—er—tough.

Lionel (*crossing to* C) I am not incapable of getting tough when necessary.

Penelope. Of course you're not, darling. Now, where did I put your flick-knife? Or perhaps Miss Skillon will lend you her bicycle chain.

Lionel (*turning to Miss Skillon; with a feeble grin*) You mustn't take any notice of Penelope, Miss Skillon. She has such a sense of humour.

Miss Skillon (*with a sour smile*) Of course not, Vicar. As if I would! (*Almost eagerly*) All the same—I'm quite sure you will have no trouble at the Institute——

(Lionel *crosses to the arch* L)

—no trouble at all, but just in case . . .

Lionel (*stopping and turning*) In case what, Miss Skillon?

Miss Skillon. Any of the young people tended to get—out of

hand; I was wondering whether perhaps if—er—one of *us*—went with you, Vicar.

PENELOPE (*innocently*) *Which* one?

MISS SKILLON. A woman's restraining influence—invaluable on such occasions.

LIONEL (*protesting*) I'm sure there is no need for either of you . . .

PENELOPE. I'm afraid it's out of the question as far as I'm concerned. (*She indicates her ankle*) My ankle . . .

MISS SKILLON (*too readily*) Yes, Mrs Toop, I'd thought of that.

PENELOPE ("*sweetly*") Of course you had. So it will *have* to be you —won't it?

LIONEL. Really, this is quite unnecessary. I can look after myself.

(IDA *bursts in excitedly from the kitchen*)

IDA (*as she enters*) Please'm . . . (*She sees Lionel and Miss Skillon. Not angrily, but in desperate exasperation*) Oooh! 'Aven't you gone *yet?*

(IDA *turns and dashes out to the kitchen*)

LIONEL (*at bursting point*) Well, upon my word! (*He turns on Penelope*) Penelope . . .

PENELOPE (*easily*) Darling, stamps or no stamps—tomorrow at the crack of dawn.

(MISS SKILLON *rises and moves to Lionel. She leaves her handbag on the table* LC)

Off you go.

MISS SKILLON. Er—shall we go, Vicar?

LIONEL. What? Oh. But, Miss Skillon, I can't let you . . .

PENELOPE (*murmuring*) What's the betting?

MISS SKILLON. I insist, Vicar.

LIONEL. I—er—I . . .

PENELOPE (*smiling at Lionel*) In any case, Lionel, you'll have to run Miss Skillon home, won't you?

LIONEL (*starting*) What?

PENELOPE. Darling, you can't possibly let her cycle home in her condition.

(MISS SKILLON *reacts*)

LIONEL (*starting*) In her . . . ?

PENELOPE (*blandly*) Minus a bulb.

LIONEL. Minus . . . ? Oh. I—er—see what . . . Ahem! (*He smiles feebly at Miss Skillon*) If I may be allowed to drive you home?

MISS SKILLON (*quickly*) Thank you, Vicar. (*She moves to* L *of the armchair*) I'm most grateful.

PENELOPE (*rising; brightly*) Then that's settled. Now, off you both go across to the Institute.

LIONEL (*testily*) Penelope, there is no need to sound so . . . It's not a *picnic* we're going on.

PENELOPE. I've a feeling it might be.

(LIONEL *glares at Penelope then turns to Miss Skillon*)

LIONEL. If you are ready, Miss Skillon . . .
MISS SKILLON (*crossing to the arch* L) Quite ready, Vicar. (*To Penelope*) May I wish you a very good night, Mrs Toop.
PENELOPE ("*sweetly*") I don't see why not. Good night.

(MISS SKILLON *glares at Penelope for a moment then sweeps out to the hall*)

LIONEL (*moving above the sofa; desperately*) Penelope, really! You are the most . . .

(PENELOPE *smiles at Lionel with genuine affection and kneels on the sofa seat at the left end*)

PENELOPE. I'm the most broad-minded wife in the world. I must be.
LIONEL (*with a sigh*) I am undoubtedly the most patient *husband.*
PENELOPE. You're a darling, and I adore you.
LIONEL (*blinking*) What?
PENELOPE. Adore you. (*She takes his hand over the back of the sofa*)
LIONEL (*melting*) Oh. Er—yes—quite. (*He smiles in spite of himself*) And do you think *I* don't adore *you* in spite of your . . . ?
PENELOPE (*snuggling up to him*) Lionel!
LIONEL (*happily*) Penelope!
PENELOPE (*firmly*) Give me a kiss. (*She puts her arms around him*)
LIONEL. A . . . ? (*He looks nervously towards the arch* L) But—Miss Skillon . . .
PENELOPE (*firmer still*) Blast Miss Skillon!
LIONEL (*shocked*) Penelope!

(PENELOPE *takes his face in her hands*)

(*Somewhat alarmed*) Oh.

(PENELOPE *pulls Lionel down on top of her, dragging his face down to hers. She holds it firmly while she gives him a long kiss, to which, in due course,* LIONEL *responds.*
MISS SKILLON *enters from the hall*)

MISS SKILLON (*seeing the kiss; with great disapproval*) Oh!

(LIONEL, *hearing Miss Skillon's "Oh!", tries to break away, but* PENELOPE *holds him deliberately and firmly in the kiss*)

(*Acidly*) Er—my bag. I left it on the table. (*She crosses to the table* LC *and picks up her handbag*)

(LIONEL *releases himself*)

LIONEL. Just saying *au revoir* to my . . .

(PENELOPE *pulls Lionel down again.* MISS SKILLON, *after a look of disapproval, crosses to the arch* L)

MISS SKILLON. I'm so sorry. Don't hurry. I can wait my turn.

(MISS SKILLON *exits to the hall.* LIONEL *releases himself*)

LIONEL (*embarrased and flustered*) Penelope—I—I—I believe you did that deliberately.
PENELOPE. I always kiss deliberately, darling—you know that.
LIONEL. You did it to shock Miss Skillon. I . . . (*With a wail*) Oh, what's the use! (*He crosses to* LC) I must go. My hat . . .

(PENELOPE *crosses, picks up Lionel's hat and puts it sideways on his head*)

The lights—you will put some of them out?
PENELOPE. Of course, darling.
LIONEL (*absently*) Bye-bye, Penelope. (*He automatically goes to kiss her*)

(PENELOPE *opens her arms*)

(*He jumps back in alarm*) No! Goodness gracious, no! Not again!

(LIONEL *exits to the hall*)

PENELOPE (*calling*) Bye-bye. (*She crosses to* R)

(IDA *dashes in from the kitchen in a state of great excitement*)

IDA (*running to the arch* L *and looking off*) Has he really gone now, mum?
PENELOPE. Yes.
IDA (*in a heartfelt mutter*) Oh, thank Gawd for that!
PENELOPE (*with an attempt at firmness*) Now, Ida, you *shouldn't* . . .
IDA (*excitedly and apologetically*) Ow'm, I *know* I shouldn't. (*She crosses to* C) Aren't I awful! But, ooh'm! (*She rushes towards Penelope almost frenziedly*) Oh'm, I'm in such a state. (*She turns, crosses and starts up the stairs*) I hardly know how to contain myself. (*She stops and turns*) I . . . Look at me! Up the stairs!
PENELOPE. Ida! Pull yourself together.
IDA (*coming down the stairs and crossing to Penelope*) I can't'm! It's too wonderful! Marvellous! You don't know what's happened, and when you do . . .
PENELOPE. What has happened, for goodness' sake?
IDA (*with almost a wail*) No'm. I mustn't tell you—not yet; not till we're sure them two's—(*she crosses and looks off* L) off the premises.
PENELOPE. What?
IDA (*crossing to* C; *excitedly*) The Vicar and Miss Skillon'm. Oh'm! I thought they'd *never* sling their 'ooks.
PENELOPE. Ida!
IDA (*excitedly apologetic*) Ow! 'Scuse me. I'll just make sure they've gone. (*She crosses to the arch* L) If I manage to live through the night . . .

(IDA *exits to the hall.* PENELOPE *gapes after her in wonderment, then smiles and limps, not too badly, to the sofa*)
IDA *dashes in from the hall*)

(*She crosses to* C; *excitedly*) They've gone'm.
PENELOPE. Then perhaps now, you'll tell me what . . .

IDA (*with an agonized wail*) No'm. Not me. You've got to hear it from Willie Briggs. (*She crosses to the kitchen door*)

PENELOPE. But, surely . . .

IDA (*crossing to* C; *desperately*) Will you come into the kitchen'm?

PENELOPE (*smiling*) No, I won't; not with *this* ankle. You can bring Willie in here.

IDA (*gaping*) In here! D'you mean that'm? Willie can come in *here?*

PENELOPE. Why not?

IDA (*excitedly*) Well! (*She goes to the kitchen door and pulls it open*) That'll just about make his day. 'Scuse me.

(IDA *dashes out to the kitchen*)

(*As she goes; calling*) Willie! Willie!

(PENELOPE *sits on the sofa.*
IDA *dashes in excitedly from the kitchen and holds the doors open*)

Willie's here'm.

PENELOPE. *Where?*

IDA (*jerking her head; indicating just outside the door*) Just here'm.

PENELOPE (*bewildered*) Well—bring him in.

IDA (*excitedly*) Yes'm. (*She turns in the doorway and speaks in an audible "sotto voce" to the unseen Willie*) Now listen, Willie Briggs! When you go in you'll remember your manners, see? And another thing—I know you're excited, but—(*with some severity*) try to look as if you belong to somebody. (*She holds the door open wide and announces*) Willie Briggs'm.

(WILLIE BRIGGS *enters from the kitchen. He is definitely a country lad, of about the same age as Ida; not very bright, but good-hearted. His clothes are countrified, there is nothing of the Teddy boy about him. He stands in the doorway nervously twiddling a beret in his hands.* IDA *is definitely "the boss" over Willie, but her bossiness is not offensive. She is actually very proud of Willie, and only anxious that he should appear to the best advantage*)

PENELOPE (*smiling encouragingly at Willie*) Good evening, Willie.

(IDA, *almost before Willie has time to reply, digs him in the ribs*)

IDA. Well, *say* something.

WILLIE (*having recovered from Ida's dig in the ribs; sheepishly to Penelope*) Ar!

IDA (*approvingly*) That's better.

PENELOPE. Sit down, Willie.

IDA (*again almost before Willie can respond to the invitation*) Well, go on. (*She pushes him a step down stage*)

WILLIE. Ar! (*He steps nervously into the room and promptly trips over his own feet. He stumbles to* C, *but does not fall*)

IDA (*crossing to* R *of Willie; admonishingly*) Well, that's a good *start off*, isn't it? (*To Penelope*) You must excuse him'm. He scarcely knows whether he's coming or going—he's that excited.

Penelope. Excited?
Ida (*excitedly*) Well, look at 'm.

(Penelope *gives a long look at the far from excited* Willie)

Penelope. I see. (*She pauses*) Well—er—do sit down.

(Willie *is about to collapse into the armchair*)

Ida (*severely*) Not there!

(Willie *quickly straightens up*)

That's Mr Toopses chair. (*She moves quickly and picks up the upright chair* L)
Penelope (*protesting but smiling*) Ida, if Willie wants to sit in that chair . . .
Ida (*bringing the chair* C; *firmly*) He'll sit on this one'm, and like it. (*She puts the chair firmly against the back of Willie's legs*)

(Willie *collapses into the chair*)

(*To Willie; firmly*) You're not a millionaire, yet, remember. (*She stands, almost in an "on guard" position* R *of Willie's chair*)

(*There is a slight pause.* Penelope *looks expectantly at* Ida *and* Willie, *but for the moment, nothing is forthcoming from them*)

Penelope (*after clearing her throat*) Well—er—(*suddenly and brightly*) Oh. (*She rises*) Can I get you a drink, Willie?
Willie. Ar!
Ida (*flatly and firmly*) *No'm.*
Penelope. Oh. Well, now—(*she sits on the sofa*) what is all this er—(*she looks at the phlegmatic Willie*) *excitement* about?
Ida. Go on, Willie. Tell Mrs Toop.

(*There is a slight pause*)

Willie (*not excitedly, but definitely*) We've come up, mum.
Ida (*rebuking him severely*) We only *think* we've come up.
Willie (*agreeing*) Ar! (*To Penelope*) We only *think* we've come up.

(Penelope *is completely out of her depth*)

Penelope (*smiling feebly at Willie*) Well, I'm—delighted—*naturally*, but, Willie—er—where do you *think* you've—*come up* from?
Willie (*blinking uncomprehendingly*) Eh?
Penelope (*mildly exasperated*) I'm sorry, but I just don't know what you're talking about.
Ida (*to Willie; severely*) You see! That's what comes of rushing.
Penelope (*putting her hand to her brow; faintly*) Rushing . . . !
Ida (*to Willie*) If you'd only take things a bit more calm. (*She moves to* L *of the sofa. Excitedly*) He means the Pools'm.
Penelope (*still not grasping*) The—er . . . ?
Ida (*desperately*) You *know*'m. What you give me sixpence every week to give to Willie for.
Penelope (*grasping*) Oh. The football Pool.

Willie. Ar!

Ida (*to Willie; sharply*) *Now* then! Tell Mrs Toop, slow. Don't fly off at a tango. (*To Penelope. Excitedly*) We've come up'm.

Willie (*to Ida*) We only *think* we've come up.

Penelope (*in despair*) Oh, my Lord! We're back where we started. (*Firmly*) Now—just a minute—let's see if I understand, shall we? Willie thinks we've won something in this Pool he's put us in. Right?

Willie. Ar!

(Ida *nods vigorously*)

Penelope (*not excited, but smiling*) Well, that's wonderful!

Ida. Yes'm.

Willie. Ar!

Penelope. Now, Willie, why don't you pop along and make sure and if we have won, bring the winnings back?

Willie (*blankly*) Pop along, ma'am? All the way to London?

Penelope (*with a start*) London? (*Befogged*) What are you talking about—*London?*

Willie (*gaping*) You said I was to pop along and collect . . .

Penelope. I *know* I did, but . . . (*She begins to get uneasy*) Ida, this —er—pool—isn't it a *local* one—run in the village?

Ida (*gaping*) In the *village*'m?

Penelope (*realizing the truth*) Good heavens! Don't tell me it's one of those commercial affairs?

(Willie *and* Ida *merely gape at Penelope*)

Oh, good heavens! (*She rises*) Mr Toop would be furious if he thought I'd dabbled in a *local* game, but if he knew I was mixed up in . . . (*Sharply*) Now look, Willie—Ida—I must have nothing to do with it.

Ida (*gaping*) Nothing to do with it?

Penelope (*firmly*) Nothing. If it got around that the Vicar's wife gambled on football Pools . . .

Ida. But'm, you . . .

Penelope (*moving to* r *of the sofa; desperately*) I thought it was just a local effort to raise funds for the cricket team or the Wolf Cubs. I had no idea . . . (*Firmer still*) If we've won something, as you seem to think—well—you must have my share.

Ida. But'm . . .

Penelope. I can't take it. I should never dare to look Mr Toop in the face again. No. (*She moves to the fireplace*) You can have my winnings; share them between you. It can go towards your Christmas present.

Ida (*weakly*) Christmas . . . !

(Penelope, *truly conscience-stricken, stands by the fireplace, facing out front, her right arm resting on the mantelpiece*)

Willie. Christmas . . . But, ma'am . . .

PENELOPE. No, no, don't thank me. (*With a little laugh*) You don't know if we've *won* anything yet. When will you know?

IDA. Tomorrow morning'm. (*She moves behind the sofa*) When Willie's seen the results in the Sunday papers. He's only checked with the wireless so far—and them announcers—they do gabble so.

PENELOPE. Checked . . . ?

IDA (*excitedly*) Yes'm. You see, Willie keeps a copy. (*To Willie*) Where is it, Willie?

WILLIE. What?

IDA. The copy?

WILLIE. Ar! (*He produces a Cope's coupon from his pocket and gives it to Ida*)

IDA. You see'm. (*She moves* R *of the sofa and gives the coupon to Penelope*) Thems all the draws and wins and things he's sent in—aren't they, Willie?

WILLIE. Ar! And only eight matches drew today.

IDA. Well'm, you see . . .

PENELOPE (*blinking at the coupon*) No, I'm afraid I don't. It just looks like—like—well, it *could* be the *Hallelujah Chorus* in Chinese for all I . . . But you say if this is right we may have won something?

IDA. Yes'm.

PENELOPE (*almost casually*) How much could it be, Willie?

WILLIE (*unexcitedly*) Well, ma'am, last week, for the same points as we've got, it was—two hundred and sixty thousand pounds . . .

PENELOPE. *What!* (*She gives a strangled croak, staggers, then turns to the fireplace with the intention of getting more support from the mantelpiece. Her right hand, which is on it already, at the downstage end, slides along to the upstage end to make room for her left hand. As her right hand travels along the mantelpiece it clears it of everything; vases, ornaments, the clock, etc., all crash to the ground. Heedless of this, she merely stands clutching each end of the mantelpiece, in a dazed condition*)

(IDA *is horrified. Even* WILLIE *is rather taken aback*)

IDA (*horrified*) Oh'm! Look what you've . . .

WILLIE (*rising and moving* C) Ooh! Ar!

(*The following action and dialogue is very quick.*

LIONEL, *very dishevelled, staggers in from the hall. He is in great mental and physical distress. His left hand covers his left eye, his right hand clutches his right knee. He is just conscious of Penelope, who, at the fireplace, is in his direct line of vision, but not of Ida and Willie.* IDA *stands aghast.* WILLIE *looks on, interested.* PENELOPE, *completely oblivious to everything that is happening, stands with her back to the room, clutching the ends of the mantelpiece*)

LIONEL (*staggering to the armchair; weakly*) Penelope . . . (*He collapses into the chair, groaning and still covering one eye*)

(MISS SKILLON *rushes in from the hall to* L *of Lionel*)

MISS SKILLON (*with much fuss*) There, there, Vicar! Be brave—be brave. *I* am here. I'll look after you.

(LIONEL *groans and raises his right hand from his knee. A large and ragged flap of his trousers leg falls down, revealing an expanse of bare and bloody knee-cap. He is about to put his right hand to his brow, but, on seeing the palm covered with blood, he gives a little howl of alarm and slides further down in the armchair*)

(*She immediately grabs Lionel's right hand and begins vigorously slapping the back of it, but not loud enough to drown the dialogue. Firmly*) Now, now, Vicar, you mustn't faint. (*She grabs a magazine from the table* LC *and fans Lionel*) Can you hear me? You mustn't . . . Oh, he *has* fainted!

(PENELOPE *turns slowly and dazedly, and faces the room. She shows no signs of having even noticed Miss Skillon or Lionel. As she turns, the crunching of broken china can be heard as she treads on the debris from the mantelpiece*)

PENELOPE (*dazedly*) Willie.

(WILLIE *and* IDA *turn to Penelope.* MISS SKILLON *concentrates on Lionel*)

(*She moves below the sofa. Slowly*) Last week, you say, it was *two hundred and sixty thousand pounds.*

WILLIE (*solemnly completing the figure*) Five shillings and fourpence (*He nods*) *Ar!*

PENELOPE. Aah! (*She collapses on to the sofa*)

MISS SKILLON *continues to pat Lionel's hand as—*

the CURTAIN *falls*

ACT II

SCENE—*The same. The following morning. 9.30 a.m.*

When the CURTAIN *rises,* IDA *is kneeling beside the fireplace with a dust-pan and brush, sweeping the hearth. She picks up the remaining pieces of china and drops them into the dustpan. There is a nude statuette lying face down on the mantelpiece.* PENELOPE *enters at the top of the stairs, carrying a tray on which there is a rather old-fashioned bedroom-type alarm clock and a number of ornaments. As she descends the stairs, the ornaments on the tray can be heard rattling. She is in a rather "nervy" state.* IDA *rises from her knees and watches Penelope.*

PENELOPE (*crossing to* C; *shakily*) Here we are, Ida.

IDA (*moving to* R *of Penelope*) Ooh'm! Your nerves! Aren't 'alf playing you up, aren't they?

PENELOPE. There isn't a nerve in my body that isn't screaming for aspirin; and I fed them all only half an hour ago. (*She holds out the tray*) Take these, Ida, before I drop them.

(IDA *takes the tray and puts it on the sofa*)

Get them dusted and put out on the mantelpiece. (*She crosses to the fireplace*) And let's just pray that Mr Toop doesn't notice the change and begin asking questions. (*She slaps the statuette*) She doesn't care, does she?

IDA. You 'aven't said anything to him yet'm about—*you* know?

PENELOPE. You mean the Pools?

(IDA *nods vigorously*)

Good heavens, no! Of course I haven't. (*She moves above the sofa*)

(IDA *picks up a duster and dusts the mantelpiece*)

IDA. And he hasn't noticed that you're—not yourself this morning?

PENELOPE. Fortunately, Mr Toop is more concerned with the fact that he isn't *him*self this morning. (*Genuinely*) I tried to get him to stay in bed, but . . . (*Alertly*) He *is* still in the kitchen having his breakfast?

IDA. Yes'm. (*She dusts the ornaments and puts them on the mantelpiece*)

(PENELOPE *crosses to the kitchen door, opens it, looks off and calls*)

PENELOPE (*with overdone brightness*) Hello-o!

(LIONEL, *off* L, *is heard to mumble*)

You—er—all right, darling?

(LIONEL *mumbles*)

(*Soothingly*) Good. Er—like some more toast? Eat your egg?

LIONEL (*off*) Don't like it.

PENELOPE. Don't like it? It's all the way from Japan.

(LIONEL *mumbles*)

Well—er—just sit quietly in there for a while. Don't try to walk about. Got your pipe?

(LIONEL *mumbles slightly louder*)

Tobacco?

(LIONEL'S *mumbling becomes more intensified*)

Darling, I'm only trying to be helpful. (*She closes the door*)

IDA. How is he, 'm?

PENELOPE. He doesn't want any more toast; he doesn't like his egg; he's got his pipe and tobacco, and would I please shut the door —there's a draught. Sounds a bit shaken up.

IDA. If he's shaken up now, he'll drop to pieces soon.

PENELOPE. Why?

IDA. When he hears about—*you* know.

PENELOPE (*with something like a wail*) A possible two hundred and sixty thousand pounds, and we have to refer to it as "*you* know". (*She crosses to* C) I shall never be able to keep silent about it, never.

IDA (*excitedly*) Ooh, neither will I.

PENELOPE (*in near panic*) Yes, you *will*, Ida.

IDA (*blinking*) But'm . . .

PENELOPE. We mustn't say a word; not to anyone—not yet. Not till Willie has found out for sure, you understand?

IDA. But'm—if I don't talk soon I shall *burst*.

PENELOPE (*almost frantically*) I'm not forbidding you to burst, only to talk.

(IDA *gapes at Penelope*)

(*She sits in the armchair*) I'm sorry, Ida. I hardly know what I'm saying.

IDA (*moving down* L *of the sofa*) I'm sure'm, that if you were to speak to the Vicar man to man . . .

PENELOPE. It's a bit too late for that.

IDA (*blinking*) Eh?

PENELOPE. Never mind. I know I shall have to talk to Mr Toop sometime, though not in the odd way you suggest; but I'm certainly not going to meet trouble half-way. We'll wait until we hear *what* we've won before I crawl to confession. (*She rises, faces front and thinks for a moment. Acting*) Can you imagine me saying to Mr Toop, "Darling—I've won eighty-six thousand, six hundred and sixty-six pounds, fifteen shillings and a penny. Can you ever forgive me?" (*She turns to Ida. Blankly*) It doesn't make sense, does it?

IDA. There's something wrong somewhere.

PENELOPE. The figure's right. I spent the night working it out.

IDA. Fancy me with all that money. (*She walks mannequin fashion to* C) I'll be able to buy myself one of them nylon fur coats, won't I, 'm?

PENELOPE. Nylon fur . . . ! (*She moves to* L *of Ida*) My dear Ida, you'll be able to buy yourself a mink for every day of the week, and a diamond tiara to clean the car in. (*She skips up* C *in delight then reacts to the injured ankle*) I can't believe it will happen. I wonder how soon we shall know.

IDA (*moving* R *and resuming work on the ornaments*) Willie's calling in on his way to church'm. Though what good he'll be in the choir today I don't know. He'll be that excited he won't be able to sing a note.

PENELOPE (*moving to the kitchen door; almost in a mutter*) Well, that will be *something*.

IDA. It seems we have to send a telegram'm.

PENELOPE (*stopping and turning*) Telegram? Who to?

IDA. Mr Cope in London. Willie wants you to help him work it out.

PENELOPE. But what's the telegram about?

IDA. To tell him we've won and ask him for the money.

PENELOPE. Is he going to like that?

IDA. But he gets telegrams every week'm.

PENELOPE. Right in the middle of his Sunday lunch? (*With a start*) And oh, my goodness! Talking of Sunday lunch—that reminds me. We have a guest.

IDA. A guest'm?

PENELOPE. Mr Toop can't possibly take the services today—not in his condition, so Mr Humphrey from St John's, Badcaster, is coming over. We shall have to feed the man—heaven help him. (*She moves to the stairs*) I'll finish off upstairs, then we must get busy in the kitchen.

IDA. Yes'm.

PENELOPE (*going up the stairs*) We're neither of us very good cooks, are we?

IDA. No'm.

PENELOPE. But what we shall do to the joint today, I shudder to think.

(PENELOPE *exits at the top of the stairs.* IDA, *while smiling at Penelope as she exits, has picked up the nude statuette. After Penelope has gone,* IDA, *about to give her mind to the job of dusting, starts when she sees the nude in her hand*)

IDA (*looking at the statuette*) Oo' you 'uzzy! (*She puts it on the mantelpiece. She then takes an old alarm clock from the tray, dusts it, shakes it, listens for the tick, then winds it. Having done this, she begins to alter the hands. Immediately the alarm goes off in a very strident and persistent ringing. She is startled by the suddenness of it*) Aah! (*She almost drops the clock, but not quite. She shakes it frantically, but, failing to stop the noise, looks at it desperately, then almost throws it on to the sofa, and quickly, too quickly, sits on it. She jumps up immediately with a cry of anguish. Her hand goes to her posterior for the briefest of moments. She then picks up the clock, which is still ringing, moves to* R *of the sofa and kneels*)

(LIONEL *enters from the kitchen. His left eye is very swollen and almost rainbow coloured. He walks with the aid of a stick. He does not see Ida kneeling* R *of the sofa. He limps as quickly as possible to the telephone. As he does so,* IDA *puts the clock under the right end of the sofa and the ringing stops abruptly as* LIONEL *lifts the receiver*)

LIONEL (*into the telephone; testily*) The Vicarage, Merton-cum-Middlewick. The Vicar speaking. (*He faces* L)

(IDA, *still on hands and knees, looks up, somewhat surprised*)

(*After a pause*) Hello? Hello? (*More testily*) Hel-lo? (*He rattles the receiver rest*)

(IDA *slides the clock under the sofa*)

Operator. Hello!

IDA (*rising behind Lionel and smiling feebly*) Hello.

LIONEL. Aah! (*Into the telephone*) Who is that speaking?

IDA. Ida.

LIONEL (*turning*) Good heavens! I didn't see you there, Ida.

IDA. I saw you.

LIONEL (*replacing the receiver*) Why didn't you answer the phone?

IDA. I—I didn't hear it.

LIONEL (*moving up* L *of the sofa*) What is the time?

(IDA *drops swiftly to her knees and retrieves the clock*)

IDA. Half past nine, as near as makes no matter. (*She slides the clock under the sofa*)

LIONEL (*turning*) When Mr Humphrey . . .

(IDA *is out of sight behind the right end of the sofa*)

What . . . ? Where are you, girl?

IDA (*rising slowly; pleasantly*) Carry on, sir—I'm with you.

LIONEL (*testily*) All this bobbing up and down. I was saying—when Mr Humphrey arrives he might like a hot drink before he goes to church.

IDA. I'll make him one, sir.

LIONEL. And please see that it *is* hot, *and* drinkable. And for heaven's sake warn him about the church bell—tell him it's been cracked since Cromwell. (*He crosses to the desk and picks up the copy of "Lady Chatterley's Lover"*)

IDA (*happily*) Yes, sir. Shame you can't take the service, in't it?

LIONEL (*crossing to the armchair*) Yes, in't it—er . . . (*He waves a hand to quieten Ida and sits in the armchair*)

IDA. Oo! It gave us quite a turn last night. I mean to say—one minute there was you and Miss Skillon skipping off as happy as sand-boys, and——

LIONEL. Skipping off?

IDA (*overlapping*) —and the *next*—there you were in that very chair—(*she points*) out for the count so to speak. (*She picks up her dust-pan and brush and brushes the carpet* R)

LIONEL (*firmly*) *Ida* . . .

IDA (*regardless*) Well, they do say, "In the midst of life we are in death."

LIONEL (*almost barking*) Where is Mrs Toop?

IDA (*vaguely*) Oh. Can't say what *she's* in the midst of; the bedrooms, I think.

LIONEL (*rising and limping towards the kitchen door*) When she comes down I want to speak to her.

IDA (*aware of his limping*) Oooh, you are a poorly soldier, aren't you, sir? Nobody can say you haven't fought the good fight.

LIONEL (*moving* C) I have fought no fight—good or bad. I fell over Miss Skillon's bicycle which she foolishly left standing outside the gate.

IDA (*crossing and sweeping the carpet* L; *muttering*) Yes—well—I suppose *somebody*'ll believe it.

LIONEL (*inwardly fuming*) I—I . . . (*He suddenly notices the new ornaments on the mantelpiece*) What on earth . . . ? (*He limps to the fireplace*) What has happened to the mantelpiece? What are all these new ornaments?

IDA (*crossing to* C) Ah! Well may you ask.

LIONEL (*putting the book on the table above the sofa*) I *am* asking.

IDA (*muttering*) And I'm telling you.

LIONEL (*not catching her remark*) What did you . . . ? (*He sees the statuette*) Good heavens! What's this woman doing here? Well, I can see what she's doing but why is she doing it on my mantelpiece? (*He picks up the statuette and gapes at it in horror*) Ida! Look at this!

(LIONEL *does not intend* IDA *to take him seriously, but she does. She crosses to* L *of Lionel and gazes at the statuette with polite interest only*)

(*After a moment; accusingly*) *Well?*

IDA (*baffled*) Well—er—you can't really expect *me* to get excited about it, can you? I mean to say, being a man, in a manner of speaking, it's natural that you should, but . . .

LIONEL (*fuming*) I—I . . . How did it get here? (*He puts the statuette on the mantelpiece*) And where are all the things that were on here yesterday?

IDA (*hedging*) Well—you see—(*she looks towards the kitchen door*) you see . . .

LIONEL (*testily*) Don't stand there telling me I see. I do *not* see.

(IDA *crosses to the waste-paper basket down* R *and empties her dustpan into it*)

IDA (*as if reproving a child*) Somebody got out of bed the wrong side this morning, didn't they, sir?

LIONEL. Ida!

(IDA *drops the dustpan into the basket and crosses to* C)

IDA (*still reproving*) Somebody who shouldn't have got out of bed at *all.*

LIONEL (*exasperated; almost shouting*) Why is the mantelpiece filled with new ornaments?

IDA (*in a sudden burst of exasperation; using Lionel's tone and volume*) 'Cos the others was knocked off.

LIONEL. Knocked off? You mean . . . ?

IDA (*picking up the tray from the sofa; shortly*) No, I *don't* mean *swiped.* They was knocked off by accident.

LIONEL (*crossing indignantly to* C) Accident! Accident indeed! (*He turns to Ida*) And there is no need to ask who had the accident, is there? (*He glares accusingly at Ida*)

(IDA *maintains a very noble silence*)

(*He misjudges the silence, turns and calls sharply up the stairs*) Penelope! Penelope! (*To Ida*) This time you have really gone too far, Ida. (*He calls loudly*) *Penelope!*

IDA (*uneasily*) Mrs Toop knows about it.

LIONEL. Mrs Toop is also going to know that *I* know about it.

(IDA *moves* R *and puts the tray on the desk*)

(*He calls*) Penelope! (*To Ida*) Mrs Toop has shielded you for the last time, my girl. (*He almost bellows*) Penelope!

PENELOPE (*off*) You calling, Lionel?

LIONEL. I am. (*He moves up* L) Will you come down here at once, please.

PENELOPE (*off*) Shan't be long, darling.

LIONEL (*loudly*) I said *at once,* Penelope.

PENELOPE (*off*) Yes, dear, but . . .

LIONEL (*firmly*) And I meant *at once.* (*He limps up* C, *muttering in high dudgeon*) It's time I asserted my authority in this house.

IDA (*dithering*) 'Course it is, sir, but don't you think you ought to insert it sitting down?

(PENELOPE *enters at the top of the stairs*)

PENELOPE (*as she enters; easily*) Now, what's all the . . . ? (*She sees Lionel limping around. Genuinely concerned*) Lionel! Your leg! You shouldn't be . . .

IDA (*wildly*) I've *told* him he shouldn't't'm.

LIONEL (*pointing an accusing finger at Penelope*) Penelope, I *know!*

PENELOPE (*stopping dead on the top stair*) *What?*

LIONEL. I've found out.

PENELOPE (*horrified*) Lionel, you *haven't?*

LIONEL. I most certainly have. Ida has confessed.

PENELOPE (*clutching the banister with both hands*) Oh, my goodness, Ida! (*She descends two steps*) How could you?

IDA (*knowing Penelope has misunderstood Lionel; frantically*) Mum! I didn't! I never!

LIONEL (*spinning round on Ida*) Do not add lying to your other misdemeanours

IDA (*stamping her foot at him; desperately*) Oh, if you'd only keep quiet, sir.
LIONEL (*advancing on Ida; outraged*) Ida!

(IDA *backs to the stool* R *and sits*)

IDA. I—I . . .
LIONEL (*moving up* C; *to Penelope, firmly*) Did you seriously think I shouldn't find out?
PENELOPE (*babbling*) Lionel—I can explain—at least, I can try. I—I . . .
IDA (*rising; with a yelp*) No'm! Don't explain! Keep him guessing.
LIONEL (*almost shouting*) Will you be silent, girl?
IDA (*desperately*) Not while there's breath in my body to utter. (*To Penelope*) Mum . . .
LIONEL (*firmly*) Penelope, I am determined that this—(*he indicates Ida*) this creature shall cause no more trouble in this house.

(IDA *grabs the statuette, looks at Penelope, points to the statuette then replaces it on the mantelpiece*)

PENELOPE (*half-way down the stairs; puzzled*) Ida? But it wasn't Ida's fault.
LIONEL. What do you mean?
PENELOPE. I grant you Ida suggested I should do it—not that I blame her for that—and I . . .
LIONEL (*gaping up at Penelope*) Ida *suggested you* should do it?

(IDA, *behind Lionel's back, makes frantic signals to attract Penelope's attention. She mimes counting money with her hands, then shakes her head vigorously. She is trying to tell Penelope that Lionel is not talking about the Pools*)

(*He turns to Ida*) Stop scratching, Ida.

(*The following business must be worked very quickly.* IDA *dives to the floor, picks up the clock and waves it frantically, pointing to it and to the mantelpiece, trying, of course, to let Penelope know it is the mantelpiece to which Lionel is referring. The clock suddenly begins ringing*)

IDA (*with a yelp*) Ow! (*She just manages to get the clock behind her back, still ringing, before Lionel turns*)
LIONEL (*turning to Ida and snapping at her*) Answer that! (*He turns to Penelope*) Penelope . . .

(IDA, *by now hardly realizing what she is doing, brings the clock from behind her and shakes it quickly and vigorously. It stops ringing. She puts it to her face as she would a telephone receiver*)

IDA (*as if answering the telephone*) Hello—hello? (*She realizes what she is doing*) Wrong number. (*She puts the clock under the sofa*)
LIONEL. Penelope, am I going completely and utterly mad? Did I understand you to say that Ida suggested you should do what you did?
PENELOPE (*desperately*) Yes, darling. Ida suggested it, and I—

well, I didn't see any harm in it, really. I thought it might be fun, so I did it.

LIONEL (*gaping*) Can I believe my ears? You thought it might be fun to knock all the ornaments off the mantelpiece, so you did it?

PENELOPE (*gaping at Lionel; blankly*) Ornaments? (*Blanker still*) Ornaments? (*She realizes what Lionel is talking about*) *Ornaments!* (*She begins to make an hysterical whinnying noise*)

LIONEL (*angrily*) Penelope!

(*The noise gets louder.* IDA *now joins in hysterically*)

(*He spins round on Ida*) *Ida!*

(IDA *collapses on the sofa*)

IDA (*between her laughing*) Ow, you'll be the death of me, mum!

LIONEL (*to Ida; sharply*) Unless you keep quiet, that will be my privilege. (*He turns to Penelope*) Penelope, I can only think you must be going out of your mind. (*He moves to the foot of the stairs*) I have never heard of such—such wanton—inexcusable behaviour in my life. To—knock ornaments off a mantelpiece because you thought it might be fun.

PENELOPE (*descending the stairs; hysterically*) Lionel, darling—what do a few ornaments matter when we stand to win . . . (*She breaks off just in time, puts her hand to her mouth and laughs*)

LIONEL (*stopping her*) Not matter? Here am I—having to scrinch and pape—er—scrache and pimp—er . . .

PENELOPE (*in almost a squeak*) Pinch and scrape. (*She crosses to the armchair, sits and laughs hysterically*)

LIONEL (*fuming*) Will you think it *fun* if I deduct ten shillings a week from your allowance until the ornaments are paid for?

PENELOPE (*her mind on the two hundred and sixty thousand pounds*) Ten shillings a week! (*She continues to laugh hysterically*)

LIONEL (*crossing to* C; *shouting*) I am inclined to make it *fifteen.*

(IDA *is squeaking with laughter*)

PENELOPE (*squeaking*) Fifteen . . . (*She tries to control herself*) Oh, Lionel, do be quiet, please.

LIONEL (*outraged*) *Penelope!* (*He turns to Ida*) And I shall most certainly stop two and sixpence a week from *your* wages, young woman.

IDA (*trying not to laugh*) Oh, sir . . .

LIONEL. Most certainly. (*Inexorably*) Two and sixpence a week from now until the third Sunday after Epiphany.

IDA (*still burbling*) But, sir . . .

LIONEL (*holding up his hand to silence her*) Not another word! (*He turns to Penelope*) Nor from you, Penelope. The subject is closed.

PENELOPE. Thank goodness!

LIONEL (*crossing to the table above the sofa*) I am going back into the kitchen. (*He picks up the book and crosses towards the kitchen door*) When Mr Humphrey arrives . . . (*He bumps his leg against the sofa. In pain*) Aaah!

IDA. Had a good trip? (*She laughs*)

(PENELOPE, *genuinely concerned, rises and moves quickly to* L *of Lionel*)

PENELOPE. Darling, you shouldn't be charging around like this. Back you go into the kitchen. Got your tobacco, pipe and matches? You know, you'd be much *safer* in *bed.*

LIONEL. But—Miss Skillon is coming to see me.

PENELOPE (*firmly*) Then you'll be safer *out* of it.

(LIONEL *exits to the kitchen*)

(*She closes the kitchen door*) Phew!

IDA (*rising and crossing to Penelope*) Ow'm! That was a near go, wasn't it? I thought you were going to let the cat out of the bag.

PENELOPE (*shuddering and crossing to* L *of the sofa*) Don't talk about it. I'm *still* covered with goose-pimples.

(LIONEL *stamps in from the kitchen*)

LIONEL (*irritably*) Where are my tobacco, pipe and matches?

PENELOPE. What? I thought we'd been through all . . .

(*The front-door bell rings*)

(*With a touch of wildness*) Ida—the front door.

IDA (*happily*) Yes'm. (*She crosses to* L) Wonder what fate 'olds in store for us now.

(IDA *exits to the hall*)

LIONEL (*exasperated*) Penelope, it's no use. That girl will have to go. "Had a good trip?" (*He imitates Ida's laugh*)

PENELOPE (*quickly*) Yes, dear, after tea. What is it you want?

LIONEL (*crossing below the sofa; testily*) My pipe, tobacco and matches. I left them on the dining-room table.

(PENELOPE *moves to* L *of Lionel and feels in his pockets*)

What are you . . . ? (*Testily*) They're not in there.

(PENELOPE *takes a copy of "Lady Chatterley's Lover" from Lionel's pocket*)

PENELOPE. Lionel!

LIONEL. I consider it my duty.

PENELOPE. So did the gamekeeper. (*She hands the book to Lionel*)

(LIONEL *puts the book in his pocket.*
IDA *dashes in from the hall and stands above the arch*)

IDA (*in an excited and hoarse whisper*) It's—(*she giggles*) it's Florence Nightingale'm.

PENELOPE. *Who?*

IDA (*speaking off*) Mr Toop's in here'm.

(MISS SKILLON *sweeps importantly in from the hall. She wears V.A.D. uniform and carries a small medical bag*)

LIONEL (*gaping*) Miss Skillon!
PENELOPE (*gaping*) I thought the war was over!

(MISS SKILLON *stops abruptly* L *of the armchair when she sees Lionel*)

MISS SKILLON (*to Lionel; almost indignantly*) What does this mean?

(PENELOPE *eyes Miss Skillon's uniform*)

LIONEL (*crossing below Penelope to* C) Yes, what does it mean?
MISS SKILLON (*ignoring Penelope; severely*) Why aren't you in bed, Mr Toop?
LIONEL. I—er—I . . .
MISS SKILLON (*putting her bag on the table* LC) You have disappointed me, Mr Toop.
PENELOPE (*sitting on the left arm of the sofa; muttering*) I'll bet he has.
MISS SKILLON (*removing her jacket; reproachfully*) You *knew* I would get here as soon as I could. (*She puts her jacket on the chair* L)
LIONEL (*dithering*) Yes, I was afraid you—I mean, I was sure you would.
MISS SKILLON. I may have my faults . . . (*She looks challengingly at Penelope*)
LIONEL. Penelope!
PENELOPE (*after a slight pause; sweetly*) I didn't say anything.
MISS SKILLON. But no-one can accuse me of neglecting a patient. (*To Ida. Sharply*) Girl! A bowl of hot water and clean towels in Mr Toop's bedroom.
IDA. What?
MISS SKILLON. At once!

(PENELOPE *rises*)

And get the bed ready.
IDA (*gaping*) You takin' him to bed?
MISS SKILLON. He should never have been allowed out of it. (*She takes a pair of rubber gloves from her bag and puts one glove on*) Someone has blundered. (*She glares at Penelope*) However, Mr Toop is going to bed, now, and he is staying there until such time as I say he may get out of it.
IDA (*ascending the stairs; muttering*) He's there for life!

(IDA *exits at the top of the stairs*)

LIONEL (*protesting feebly*) Miss Skillon—I hardly think it necessary . . . (*To Penelope. Despairingly*) Penelope . . .
MISS SKILLON (*moving to* L *of Lionel*) Mr Toop, *I* am in charge, if you don't mind. (*She blows the second glove in his face*)

(LIONEL *backs above Penelope to* R *of her.* PENELOPE *enjoys all this*)

(*She puts on the second glove*) Unless your leg and that cut on your forehead have proper treatment we look like having to cope with septicaemia.
LIONEL (*despairingly*) I think I'd rather cope with *that* than . . .

MISS SKILLON (*humouring him; with a firm smile*) Now we are not going to be difficult, are we?

PENELOPE. Of course we aren't. (*To Lionel*) Darling, I expect mother knows be—er—Miss Skillon knows best.

MISS SKILLON. Thank you, Mrs Toop. (*She takes a stethoscope from her bag and puts it round her neck*) I'm *sure* I do.

PENELOPE (*brightly*) You see, Lionel? So there's nothing more to be said. Now, off you both go. I must see about lunch.

LIONEL. Penelope!

PENELOPE (*crossing to the kitchen door*) Will you—er—still be here at lunch-time, Miss Skillon?

MISS SKILLON (*smiling austerely at Lionel*) That will depend on how we are getting along, won't it?

PENELOPE (*with a look*) I see what you mean—exactly.

(PENELOPE *exits to the kitchen*)

LIONEL (*as Penelope exits; it is a cry from the heart*) Penelope . . . (*He backs below the sofa*)

MISS SKILLON (*advancing on Lionel*) I must say Mrs Toop takes your condition very lightly.

(LIONEL *stumbles and falls on to the sofa at the left end*)

(*She crosses to* R *of Lionel*) I don't think she realizes how serious it is. (*She sits* R *of Lionel on the sofa*) That head—let me look at it. (*She examines Lionel's head*) I don't like that.

LIONEL (*in pain; clutching his leg*) Neither do I.

MISS SKILLON. And that leg. (*She grabs Lionel's right leg, puts it on her lap and holds it above the knee*)

LIONEL (*in alarm*) Miss Skillon—I beg of you! Really, if the Bishop were to walk in . . .

(MISS SKILLON *feels his leg with both hands*)

(*He squirms*) *Miss* Skillon!

MISS SKILLON. Just as I thought. We're going to have to work on this.

LIONEL (*wincing with pain*) Aah!

MISS SKILLON. Look me in the eye, Mr Toop.

LIONEL. I can't—not ever again.

MISS SKILLON. Straight in the eye.

(LIONEL *looks at Miss Skillon*)

(*She studies his eye*) Horrible!

LIONEL. Ghastly!

MISS SKILLON. We look like having trouble. (*She works his leg up and down*)

LIONEL. I feel that, too.

(MISS SKILLON *feels the leg.* LIONEL *laughs hysterically*)

MISS SKILLON (*putting the stethoscope into her ears*) We are not—by any chance—feeling light-headed? We're not concussed?

LIONEL. *I'm* not.
MISS SKILLON. What?
LIONEL (*taking the cup of the stethoscope and speaking into it*) I'm not.

(MISS SKILLON *reacts*)

MISS SKILLON. I shouldn't be surprised if this doesn't put you flat on your back. We'll look on the bright side, shall we?

(IDA *enters down the stairs*)

(*She sees Ida, rises, still holding Lionel's leg*) Ah! Is the bedroom ready? (*She drops the leg*)
IDA. And waiting.
MISS SKILLON (*crossing to* C) Good!
IDA (*muttering*) I wonder?
MISS SKILLON (*to Lionel*) Into bed we go. (*She collects her bag and jacket*)

(LIONEL *reacts*)

IDA. And a good time will be 'ad by all.

(IDA *exits to the kitchen*)

MISS SKILLON. Ready, Vicar? (*She crosses to him*)
LIONEL (*rising*) Miss Skillon—(*he turns away* R)

(MISS SKILLON *grabs Lionel's arm*)

—I'm sure you mean well, but—I really must point out—what I mean is—er—is it quite—er—quite right that you—after all—you are one of my parishioners—and—er . . .
MISS SKILLON. I am also your nurse, Mr Toop. (*She swings him to* C *and leads him to the stairs*)
LIONEL. Er—quite—but what will the world say?
MISS SKILLON. My uniform is my protection.
LIONEL. Miss Skillon, I assure you, you will not need your uniform.
MISS SKILLON. What?
LIONEL. I mean—protecting. (*He goes up the stairs*)
MISS SKILLON (*following Lionel up the stairs*) It must be clearly understood; from now on friendship must be put aside. You are my patient. I am your nurse. You must not think of me as a woman.
LIONEL. I never have.

(LIONEL *and* MISS SKILLON *exit at the top of the stairs.*
IDA *enters from the kitchen carrying a bowl and a towel, and moves to the stairs.*
WILLIE *appears outside the french windows. He carries a Sunday paper*)

WILLIE (*tapping on the window*) Yoo-hoo.

(IDA *puts the bowl and towel on the chair up* C *and opens the french windows*)

(*He comes into the room*) I've got the paper.

IDA (*closing the windows*) Have we won?

WILLIE. I dunno, Mrs Toop's got the coupon.

(PENELOPE *enters from the kitchen. She carries a mixing bowl and spoon*)

PENELOPE. Have we won?

IDA. We dunno, you've got the coupon.

PENELOPE. I haven't got it, he's got it.

IDA (*to Willie*) You've got it.

WILLIE. I haven't got it.

IDA (*horrified*) Perhaps Mr Toop's got it.

(WILLIE *crosses to the fireplace*)

PENELOPE (*turning to go*) I'll go and . . . (*She stops and turns*) Don't be silly, Ida. Willie—you must have it.

WILLIE. No, mum.

PENELOPE (*crossing to Willie*) When did you last see your coupon?

WILLIE. I had it here, mum, last night.

PENELOPE. Then it must still be here.

IDA. Let's look for it—you never know. (*She searches in the armchair*)

PENELOPE (*putting the bowl on the desk*) This Yorkshire pudding will never be done today.

(WILLIE *goes on all fours and looks around the sofa*)

(*She searches in the waste-paper basket*) Ida, did you turn this room out this morning?

IDA. Yes'm. In a manner of speaking. (*She searches on the bookshelves* L)

PENELOPE. And you didn't see anything of Willie's form?

IDA. No'm.

PENELOPE (*crossing to* C) Then, Willie, you must have it on you—somewhere.

WILLIE (*rising*) But'm, I'm sure I . . .

IDA. Willie Briggs, don't argue. Mrs Toop knows what she's talking about.

PENELOPE (*indicating his suit*) Have you been through all your pockets, Willie?

WILLIE. No'm, 'cos . . .

IDA (*crossing to Willie; excitedly*) We'll go through 'em, now, bonehead.

PENELOPE (*reprovingly*) Ida, is that kind?

IDA. No'm. It wasn't meant to be kind.

WILLIE. "Sticks and stones may break my bones, but . . ."

IDA. We've no time for poetry. (*She tears Willie's jacket off*) Off with that!

WILLIE (*alarmed*) Oooh! Ar! Ooh! (*To Penelope*) She'll 'ave to marry me, now.

PENELOPE. I'll see she does.

Ida (*handing the jacket to Penelope*) Will you go through that'm? Bein' married you'll 'ave 'ad more practice.

Penelope (*with dignity*) Ida, are you suggesting . . . ? (*She concentrates on the jacket*) They usually make a slit in the lining hoping you won't think to feel down there.

Willie (*to Penelope; anxiously*) You didn't ought to go through them pockets'm. You don't know what you might . . .

(Ida *strips Willie of his waistcoat*)

Aaah!

Ida. Off with it!

Willie (*grinning*) Eee! Striptease!

Penelope (*turning to face Willie; alarmed*) What?

Willie (*grinning broadly*) I'm game! (*He begins to slip his braces over his shoulders*)

Ida / Penelope (*together*) No, Willie, no!

Willie (*replacing his braces*) No'm?

Penelope. Definitely *not.*

(Ida *sits in the armchair and examines the waistcoat*)

(*She puts her hand in a pocket of the jacket*) Errr! (*With horror*) Willie—what on earth . . . ? (*She takes out a sticky paper bag*) Good heavens! Humbugs!

Willie. They're for first lesson. You can 'ave *one* if you like.

Penelope (*gazing into the bag*) They look as if they've *been* had once, already. (*She replaces the bag in the pocket*)

Ida. All he thinks about'm is 'is stomach.

Penelope (*taking an "Art" magazine from another pocket*) That's what you think. (*She sits on the sofa and looks at the magazine*) "*Continental Art Studies.*" Willie!

Willie (*placidly*) Ar! They're for *second* lesson.

Penelope (*looking at a picture*) She *must* be deformed.

Ida (*rising, crossing to Penelope and taking the magazine*) Let me see that'm. (*She looks at a picture. With a little scream*) Oooh! *Look* at 'er! It's working on a farm, that's what does it to 'im; bein' among all them animals.

Penelope. I see your point.

Ida (*giving the book to Willie*) Get rid of that. (*She puts the waistcoat on the sofa*) Now, go through your trousers. (*She crosses to the bookshelves* L.)

Willie. Ar!

Penelope (*putting the jacket on the sofa*) Well, there's no form here.

Willie. I could have told you that, m'm, but you wouldn't listen. 'Tain't likely there would be.

Ida (*crossing to* C) Why not?

Willie. 'Cos I weren't wearing this suit last night. (*He laughs and sits in the armchair*)

Penelope. Oh, Willie. Come on, let's turn out this room from top to bottom. There's two hundred and sixty thousand pounds at stake. (*She crosses to the desk and searches in it*)

(IDA *returns to the bookshelves* L *and searches*)

IDA (*to Willie*) And you.

(WILLIE *rises, goes to the downstage end of the bookshelves* L *and searches.*
The REVEREND ARTHUR HUMPHREY *enters from the hall*)

HUMPHREY. Good morning.

(WILLIE *moves and searches in the armchair*)

Good morning.

(WILLIE *throws out the cushion from the armchair and it hits Humphrey in the face*)

IDA (*turning to Willie and indicating the magazine*) Get rid of that.
HUMPHREY. I wonder if I could see . . . ?

(WILLIE *hands the magazine to Humphrey*)

Oh! (*He moves to* R *of Ida*) I wonder if I could see Mr Toop.
IDA. I'm afraid you can't, he's just gone to bed.
HUMPHREY. Oh!
IDA. With Miss Skillon.
HUMPHREY. Oh! (*He crosses to Penelope*) Ah! Mrs Toop! I wonder if I could . . . ?
PENELOPE (*picking up the bowl*) You must excuse me, I've got rather a lot on my mind at the moment. (*She hands the bowl to Humphrey and crosses to* C)
HUMPHREY. You must have.
PENELOPE (*turning, stopping and recognizing him*) Mr Humphrey! (*She turns to Ida*) Ida, that dress I was wearing last night, go and see if it's in there. Willie, come and help me look in the kitchen.

(IDA *exits up the stairs.*
WILLIE *exits to the kitchen*)

Mr Humphrey, do you like Yorkshire pudding?
HUMPHREY. No.
PENELOPE. Good.

(PENELOPE *exits to the kitchen.* HUMPHREY, *left alone, is still holding the pudding bowl. He tries to put it under the sofa, then puts it on the desk. He puts his bag on the sofa at the right end, his hat on the table behind the sofa, then sits* C *of the sofa. As he sits there is an enormous crash from the kitchen, accompanied by cries from* WILLIE. HUMPHREY *leaps up*)

HUMPHREY. Heaven moves in a mysterious way. (*He sits on the sofa*)

(The alarm clock rings. Humphrey *leaps up and runs around the sofa, trying to locate the source of the sound. Eventually he finds the clock under the sofa, picks it up and hits it with his hand. The alarm stops)*

(He puts the clock on the mantelpiece) What an extraordinary place to put an alarm clock. *(He puts his hand in his pocket and, after searching for a few moments, pulls out a Pools coupon and sits on the sofa)* Aston Villa —Birmingham . . . Oh, of course, a newspaper, to check. *(He rises, searches for a newspaper on the desk, crosses to the bookshelves* L, *then returns to the sofa, kneels at the left end and looks under it)*

(Ida *enters down the stairs)*

Ida *(crossing to* L *of Humphrey)* On your knees already? You are keen, aren't you? Got all you want?

Humphrey *(holding out the coupon)* I was looking for a paper to check my . . . *(Then, in horror, he quickly stuffs the form under the cushion and corrects himself)* To *read.*

Ida *(picking up a paper from the table* LC*)* Well, here's the *Church Times. (She holds the paper out to Humphrey)* Couldn't be better, could it?

Humphrey. That doesn't give the . . . I've already read it.

Ida. Well, now—*(with a quick look towards the stairs)* if you won't tell Mr Toop I gave it to you, I could let you have last week's *War Cry.*

Humphrey. You—er—you don't happen to have a copy of—say —the *News of the World?*

Ida *(with mock horror)* Oooh! *Mis*ter Humphrey. *(She gives him a gentle push)*

(Humphrey *falls forward on his hands)*

Aren't you a one!

Humphrey *(babbling)* I—I—please . . . *(He rises)* You don't understand. I—I . . .

Ida. Nor wouldn't Mr Toop if he heard you. He won't have *any* Sunday papers, but—the *News of the World. Oo! Mis*ter Humphrey.

Humphrey *(embarrassed)* You don't understand. I only wanted to look at the—at the . . .

Ida *(placatingly)* 'Course you did. And why *shouldn't* you? You're flesh and blood, aren't you?—with 'ot human passions.

Humphrey. 'Ot what?

Ida. Tell you what, though. Willie, that's my boy friend, he always gets it. He's in the choir.

Humphrey. How gratifying.

Ida. Isn't it? And he takes it to church with him. Says it passes the time during the sermon.

(Humphrey *reacts)*

Well—he can lend it to you, and you can 'ave a quick look through it in the vestry then slip it back to Willie during one of the hymns.

Humphrey. I—I . . . Well—really!

IDA. It's all right, he sits next to you so the congregation won't notice. They're blind as bats, anyway—all three of 'em. (*She crosses and puts the "Church Times" on the desk*)

(PENELOPE *and* WILLIE *enter from the kitchen*)

PENELOPE (*moving down* C) Any luck, Ida?
IDA. No, mum.

(WILLIE *moves down* LC, *picks up the cushion and replaces it in the armchair*)

PENELOPE. Well, it's not in the kitchen so it must be in here. We'll just have to turn everything in this room upside down.

(*They all look at* HUMPHREY, *who is terrified*)

Would you like to go upstairs?
HUMPHREY. Why?
PENELOPE. You must want a wash before you go to church. You know where the bathroom is? Second on the left.
HUMPHREY (*crossing to the stairs*) Thank you. If you think it advisable.
PENELOPE. Oh, I do. You'll find it's a very long service. The choir are terribly slow on the psalms and hymns.
HUMPHREY (*going up the stairs*) Oh, I see what you mean. You did say the second on the left?
PENELOPE. Yes, not the first, my husband and Miss Skillon are in there.
HUMPHREY. Oh, quite—er . . .

(HUMPHREY *reacts and exits at the top of the stairs*)

PENELOPE. That's got rid of him—now we can get on with it. (*She suddenly sniffs*) Ida, can you smell burning?
IDA. Yes'm.
WILLIE (*sniffing*) Meat.
PENELOPE. The joint. It's on a high gas. Should be on a low.

(PENELOPE *dashes off into the kitchen*)

IDA. Now we've lost the joint, as well. Don't stand there like a stuffed dummy, Willie Briggs. (*She picks up his jacket and waistcoat from the sofa and crosses to Willie*) Get your waistcoat on again—and your jacket. (*She holds the waistcoat out to him*)

(WILLIE, *not realizing it, puts his arms through the waistcoat, back to front*)

WILLIE (*laughing*) 'Ad Mrs Toop proper, didn't I, 'bout my suit? Proper scream that were.
IDA (*seeing what Willie is doing*) Not that way. (*She helps him reverse the waistcoat and fastens the buttons*) I don't know what's come over you, Willie.
WILLIE. Ar! Proper sharp, aren't I? (*He puts on his jacket*) 'Taint like me.

Ida. It's the thought of all this money—it's doing things to you and we haven't *got* it yet. And the way things are going it doesn't look as if we ever shall. (*She makes a further search in the desk*) Oh, do look for that form, Willie. (*With a wail*) It must be here, somewhere. (*She moves to search on the sofa, lifts a cushion and sees Humphrey's coupon. Excitedly*) What's this? Willie! It's here. (*She picks up the coupon*)

Willie (*crossing to Ida*) Oooh! Ah! Ooh!

Ida. I've found it. (*She hands the coupon to Willie*) It is it, isn't it?

Willie (*looking quickly at the coupon*) Ar! That's it all right.

Ida (*ecstatically*) Oh, Willie, aren't I wonderful! (*She flings her arms around Willie and spins him round*)

(Willie *overbalances on to the sofa*)

(*She falls on top of him*) Aaah!

(Humphrey *enters at the top of the stairs*)

Willie (*his arms around Ida; thoroughly enjoying himself*) Ar! Oooh! Ar!

(Humphrey *comes half-way down the stairs then stops and gapes, horrified*)

Ida. Willie, give over; stop it. (*She frees herself and kneels on the sofa, with her back to Humphrey*) The very idea! (*She points to the coupon*) And put that thing away before anybody sees it.

(Humphrey *starts and begins to retreat up the stairs*)

(*She rises and sees Humphrey*) Oh, Mr Humphrey.

Humphrey (*stopping*) I beg your pardon—am I in the way?

(Lionel, *dishevelled and slightly hysterical, enters at the top of the stairs. He is minus his trousers and has a tartan travelling rug draped around him*)

(*He sees Lionel*) Good heavens, Mr Toop!

Lionel. Mr Humphrey!

Humphrey (*startled by Lionel's appearance*) But—er—what . . . ?

Lionel (*descending towards Humphrey*) Mr Humphrey—take me away. Take me away.

Humphrey (*backing down the stairs*) Take you . . . ? But my very dear sir . . .

(Lionel *descends the stairs, forcing* Humphrey *to back down in front of him*)

Lionel. My very dear Humphrey—that woman—she's locked up my trousers. You don't know—you don't know what she wants to do to me. She wants to . . .

Humphrey (*wildly*) No! Don't tell me.

Lionel. She wants to put my leg in splints.

Humphrey. Oh! But, Mr Toop . . .

Lionel. I must get out of her clutches. I must hide from her.

Humphrey (*dazed*) Hide?

(*They have both reached the bottom of the stairs*)

LIONEL. You don't know her, Mr Humphrey. She means well. (*Desperately*) Where can I go? (*He moves to the arch* L)

HUMPHREY. Where would you like to go?

LIONEL (*moving to Humphrey and clutching him; pleadingly*) Mr Humphrey, help me—help me.

HUMPHREY (*babbling*) Of course, of course, but what . . . ?

LIONEL (*clinging to him beseechingly*) Take me to the potting shed.

HUMPHREY. The potting . . . ?

LIONEL. Now—at once—she won't think to look for me there. (*Desperately*) Please, Mr Humphrey—the potting shed.

HUMPHREY. But I—I . . . You're not dressed for the potting shed.

LIONEL (*indicating the cupboard with a brief gesture*) There must be something I can wear there.

HUMPHREY. Wear where?

LIONEL (*pushing Humphrey towards the cupboard*) In the cupboard. Hurry, man. Miss Skillon will be back in my bedroom at any minute now, and . . .

MISS SKILLON (*off upstairs; in alarm*) Mr Toop! Mr Toop! Where are you?

LIONEL (*terrified*) Aaaah! She . . .

(MISS SKILLON *enters at the top of the stairs.*

LIONEL *darts into the cupboard, pushing* HUMPHREY *further in and quickly closing the door after them*)

MISS SKILLON (*quickly descending the stairs and calling*) Mr Toop! Mr Toop! (*To Ida*) Girl! Where is Mr Toop?

IDA. Mr Toop'm?

MISS SKILLON. He isn't in his bedroom.

IDA. P'raps he's in the . . .

MISS SKILLON. He is not. I've just been there myself.

IDA. I was thinking of his den.

MISS SKILLON. He isn't upstairs at all. I've looked everywhere.

IDA. Funny, isn't it?

MISS SKILLON. It is far from funny. Mr Toop is not fit to be left alone. He has all the symptoms of amnesia.

IDA (*crossing to* C) I 'ad a bout of that last week—in my arm.

MISS SKILLON (*moving to* L *of the armchair*) Don't talk nonsense, girl. He must have come downstairs. Didn't you see him?

IDA. No'm.

MISS SKILLON (*to Willie*) Nor you?

IDA (*firmly*) No'm.

MISS SKILLON (*moving to the hall and calling*) Mr Toop! Mr Toop!

(MISS SKILLON *exits to the hall. From now until the end of the Act the scene gathers speed and momentum.*

PENELOPE *enters from the kitchen, coughing and red-eyed. Her hair is somewhat awry and there is a suggestion of dabs of soot on her face. She stands just inside the door, coughing and wiping her eyes.*

MISS SKILLON *re-enters from the hall*)

(*She moves to Penelope*) Mrs Toop, your husband . . .

PENELOPE. Burnt to a frazzle.

MISS SKILLON (*with a start*) *Mr Toop* burnt to a frazzle?

PENELOPE (*exasperated*) Miss Skillon, you have a one-track mind. I'm talking about the Sunday joint. (*She paces up* C *and back*) Burnt to a cinder. The kitchen blue with smoke. What am I going to do? *Five* people to feed and . . .

MISS SKILLON (*almost shouting*) Your husband has *disappeared.*

PENELOPE. *Four* people to feed—and nothing to feed them on. (*She paces up* C *and back*)

MISS SKILLON (*following Penelope*) Mrs Toop—will you listen to me? I am trying to tell you . . .

PENELOPE. Miss Skillon—without wishing to be anti-social—the only thing I want you to tell me is that you won't be here for lunch.

MISS SKILLON. I shall not leave this house until my patient is found.

PENELOPE (*with a wail*) That means you *will* be. Well, you'll just have to make do with Yorkshire pudding.

MISS SKILLON (*moving down* L; *fuming*) Of course, I always knew theatre people were mad, but . . . I tell you *again*, Mrs Toop, your husband has disappeared from his bedroom. He is in a dangerous condition . . .

PENELOPE (*crossing to* L *of the sofa*) Ida, do you think your mother could lend us a tin of corned beef?

MISS SKILLON (*fuming*) Corned beef? Mrs Toop!

IDA (*happily*) I could go and find out, couldn't I, 'm?

PENELOPE. Miss Skillon, will you lend Ida your bicycle?

MISS SKILLON. If that girl touches my bicycle, I'll . . .

PENELOPE. You'll have to walk, Ida, but for heaven's sake remember we want it for lunch—not supper.

MISS SKILLON (*moving above the armchair*) I am going to search every room in this house, Mrs Toop, and if I can't find the Vicar I shall organize a search party.

PENELOPE (*almost wildly*) Do, do. But for heaven's sake don't bring them here for a meal.

MISS SKILLON (*fuming*) Oooooh!

(MISS SKILLON *stamps off to the kitchen.* PENELOPE *moves to the armchair and sits.* WILLIE *moves to the mantelpiece and gazes at the statuette*)

PENELOPE (*with relief*) Oh, thank heaven! (*She clutches her head*) At last I can begin to attempt to think.

IDA (*eagerly*) No'm, don't think yet. Not till we've shown you, eh, Willie? Willie!

(WILLIE *turns*)

(*She dashes to the sofa and picks up Humphrey's coupon*) We've found it.

PENELOPE. What . . . ?

IDA. The *copy*'m. Now we can see if we've won all that money.

PENELOPE. I'd give my share to anybody who could produce two pounds of rump steak.

IDA. Willie—got your newspaper to check with?

WILLIE (*producing a much-folded newspaper from his pocket*) Ar!

IDA. Well, come on—what are we waiting for?

(*Two very cracked church bells begin to ring.* WILLIE *crosses to* C *and points his thumb towards the french windows, indicating the bells*)

WILLIE. Church! I'll 'ave to go. My turn to do the hymn-boards.

IDA. But we've *got* to know . . .

PENELOPE (*desperately*) Not *now*, Ida. (*She rises*) The corned beef.

WILLIE (*taking the coupon from Ida and stuffing it into his pocket with the newspaper*) I'll check it in the sermon. Got a pencil?

IDA (*excitedly*) Pencil—pencil . . . (*She gets a pencil from the desk and gives it to Willie*)

WILLIE. I'll have to hurry.

PENELOPE (*pushing Willie to the french windows*) Go this way.

(WILLIE *exits by the french windows.* PENELOPE *closes the windows* IDA *crosses to the kitchen door. Unseen by the others,* HUMPHREY'S *head comes round the cupboard door, then retires quickly as the kitchen door opens.*

MISS SKILLON *marches in from the kitchen. The cupboard and kitchen doors open at the same time, trapping* IDA *between them*)

MISS SKILLON (*as she enters*) Not a sign of him. Mrs Toop, I am going to institute a search.

PENELOPE (*desperately*) Miss Skillon, will you please . . .

MISS SKILLON. Mrs Toop, if your husband means nothing to *you*, *he* does to me.

PENELOPE (*moving to* R *of Miss Skillon*) I think you should stop and consider precisely what you mean to *him*.

MISS SKILLON. My reputation with the brigade is at stake. It is absolutely forbidden for a member to lose her patient. (*She crosses to the french windows, opens them and calls*) Stop that bell!

PENELOPE (*gaping*) What?

MISS SKILLON (*turning to Penelope*) There will be no service until Mr Toop is found. This is an emergency. Priority number one. I'll muster the whole village if need be. (*She turns and calls out of the french windows*) Stop that bell!

(MISS SKILLON *exits by the french windows*)

PENELOPE (*moving to the french windows*) For heaven's sake. (*She clutches her head*)

(IDA *moves* LC)

(*She turns to Ida*) Ida! What about that corned beef?

IDA. Just going'm. (*She moves to the french windows*) Won't it be wonderful when we get that money'm? We'll *stock* the larder with corned beef, won't we'm?

(IDA *exits by the french windows.* PENELOPE *moves to the sofa.*
HUMPHREY *cautiously opens the cupboard door, puts his head round, then squeezes himself through as little space as possible and closes the door behind him. He moves forward a step or two.* PENELOPE *is about to collapse on to the sofa*)

HUMPHREY (*apprehensively*) Mrs Toop . . .
PENELOPE (*starting*) What? (*She turns. Dazedly*) Why—Mr Humphrey! I think you ought to get across to the church at once.
HUMPHREY (*pointing to the cupboard*) Your husband . . .
PENELOPE. Miss Skillon is planning to sabotage your service, and we can't have that, can we?
HUMPHREY. Mrs Toop . . . (*He points, very vaguely, to the cupboard*)
PENELOPE (*unheeding*) Now, where are your "props"? I saw them somewhere. (*She picks up Humphrey's bag and gives it to him*) Now, you know the short cut? (*She leads Humphrey to the french windows*) The end of the garden—through the little gate and it brings you to the vestry door. Bye-bye—good luck. I'm sure you'll have a *big* success.
HUMPHREY (*dazed*) I—I—er . . .

(HUMPHREY *gapes at Penelope then totters off by the french windows.* PENELOPE *moves dazedly towards the kitchen door. The telephone rings*)

PENELOPE (*with an almost hysterical wail*) Oh, no! (*She crosses to the telephone and lifts the receiver*)

(*The church bells stop ringing*)

(*Into the telephone. Rather desperately*) The Vicarage, Merton-cum-Middlewick. Mrs Toop speaking . . . Who? . . . (*With almost horrified surprise*) Uncle Dudley? . . . But what . . . ? Where are you? . . . Badcaster? . . .

(*At this point, several small* CHOIRBOYS *in cassocks and surplices are seen crossing outside the french windows, calling out "Mr Toop", "Mr Too-oop". One or two are giving scout calls by "oohing" loudly and wobbling a finger up and down in the mouth. All are thoroughly enjoying themselves as they search for the Vicar. If it is impossible to have choir-boys, shouts only will have to be substituted, but* WILLIE, *in cassock and surplice, could be used.*
MISS SKILLON *also passes the window, issuing orders*)

MISS SKILLON (*as she passes*) Look everywhere, boys. Everywhere. Not a blade of grass must be left unturned.

(*There are yells of delight and more shouts of "Mr Too-oop" and the* BOYS *are seen running hither and thither. The noise in the garden is quite loud.* PENELOPE, *at the telephone, turns and looks horrified at what is going on in the garden*)

PENELOPE (*into the telephone*) I'm sorry, Uncle darling, I can't hear what you . . . All hell is being let loose here . . . (*Loudly*) *Hell—you* know—(*she spells*) H, E, double L . . . No, I can't explain . . . You see, there are . . . (*Frantically*) There are choirboys at the bottom of our garden . . . What was that you said? . . . (*With horror*) Coming on here . . . (*Frantically*) For lunch? . . . Darling, when? . . . (*Horrified*) Right away! But that means . . . (*With sudden wildness*) No, no, Uncle! You mustn't! . . .

(*There are more shouts, yells and running in the garden*)

(*She almost shouts*) Uncle, don't ring off—and don't come for . . . Uncle! Uncle! (*She jabs the receiver rest frantically up and down*) Uncle —for pity's sake . . . (*She realizes he has rung off and replaces the receiver, stunned. To herself, in a dead voice*) He's coming to lunch—the Bishop. (*She counts flatly on her fingers*) That's one—two—three—four . . .

(*The cupboard door opens slowly and* LIONEL *is seen standing in the doorway*)

LIONEL (*dazedly*) Penelope . . .

(PENELOPE *turns and sees Lionel, but with her mind on the food problem, she crosses to the cupboard*)

PENELOPE (*piteously*) Lionel—darling—*please*—*not* until after lunch.

PENELOPE *slowly closes the door, shutting* LIONEL *in the cupboard and exits to the kitchen. The yells in the garden burst out once more.* MISS SKILLON *leads the* CHOIRBOYS *in through the french windows and acrcss to the hall as—*

the CURTAIN *falls*

ACT III

SCENE—*The same. Fifteen minutes later.*

When the CURTAIN *rises, the room is empty. The french windows are open. There is a Red Cross tin and flags on the floor below the armchair.* WILLIE, *off in the garden is heard "Yoo-hooing" with his finger in his mouth. After a moment,* WILLIE, *now in choirboy's cassock, surplice and large ruff, dashes in by the french windows. He stands for a moment, uncertain, then goes to the kitchen door and opens it.*

WILLIE (*calling cautiously*) Ida! Ida! (*On receiving no reply, he inserts his finger in his mouth and, wobbling it up and down, "yoo-hoos" loudly*)

(MISS SKILLON *enters by the french windows. She does not see Willie. She is carrying an ordnance map and a telescope. On hearing Willie's "yoo-hoo" she turns, looks out of the french windows through her telescope, inserts her finger in her mouth and "yoo-hoos" Willie-fashion.* WILLIE *looks up blankly.* MISS SKILLON *is hidden from him. When she has finished "yoo-hooing",* WILLIE *immediately takes it up, still standing by the kitchen door. There follows a series of "yoo-hoos", long and short from* MISS SKILLON *and* WILLIE. *At last,* MISS SKILLON *calls into the garden*)

MISS SKILLON (*calling*) Come here! Whoever and wherever you are. Come and report to me.

(WILLIE, *unseen by* MISS SKILLON, *moves and stands behind her*)

I'm moving my base. (*She again "yoo-hoos"*)

(*As* MISS SKILLON *finishes "yoo-hooing",* WILLIE *immediately "yoo-hoos" behind her back.* MISS SKILLON *leaps round with a cry of surprise*)

Briggs!

WILLIE. Ar!

MISS SKILLON. What are you . . .? Why are you . . . ? (*Eagerly*) Have you found Mr Toop?

WILLIE. No'm.

MISS SKILLON (*moving down* C) Then why are you shilly-shallying here?

(WILLIE *moves to* R *of* MISS SKILLON, *who kneels and spreads her map on the floor.* WILLIE *kneels* R *of her*)

You should be searching with the others.

WILLIE. Can't think of no place else to look.

MISS SKILLON. I'll find you somewhere. (*She looks at the map*) Now—have you searched Merton Wood?

WILLIE. Ar!

MISS SKILLON (*after sticking a flag in the map*) And the Long Spinney?
WILLIE. Ar!

(MISS SKILLON *sticks another flag into the map*)

MISS SKILLON. What about—er—Lovers' Lane?

(WILLIE *forgets himself for the moment and gives Miss Skillon a knowing little push on the shoulders*)

WILLIE (*grinning*) Ar!
MISS SKILLON. *Briggs!*
WILLIE (*with a wink*) He ain't down there.
MISS SKILLON (*restraining herself and consulting the map*) There's Middlewick Pond.
WILLIE (*with a start*) Think he's in there?
MISS SKILLON. There's the shrubbery round it. That must be your next objective. If Mr Toop is not there, *you* report back here to me. (*She looks at the map*) I—in the meantime, will arrange to bivouac.

(PENELOPE *enters from the kitchen, carrying a small tray on which there is a cup of coffee*)

PENELOPE (*with a little guilty start on seeing the others*) Oh! (*She quickly recovers*) Oh, Willie, thank goodness you're . . . (*She quickly puts the tray on the table* LC *and crosses to* R *of Willie*) Will you be an angel and go after Ida, and ask her . . . ?
MISS SKILLON (*still on her knees; firmly*) Briggs is already fully occupied, Mrs Toop.

(WILLIE *rises*)

PENELOPE. But this is important, Miss Skillon. (*She leads Willie to the french windows*) Ask Ida if she . . .
MISS SKILLON. And the fact that your husband is missing—that is *not* important?
PENELOPE. Not in the least——

(MISS SKILLON *looks away with an "Oh!" of disgust*)

—(*with a quick look towards the cupboard; muttering*) so long as he stays that way.
MISS SKILLON. Not important!
PENELOPE (*to Willie; confidentially*) Ask Ida, if she can, to get *two* tins of corned beef. Tell her we have a guest for lunch.
MISS SKILLON. Mrs Toop . . .
PENELOPE. Off you go, Willie. (*She pushes him out of the french windows*) And do hurry, there's a darling.
WILLIE (*happily*) Ar!

(WILLIE *exits by the french windows*)

MISS SKILLON (*rising; fuming*) Mrs Toop, this is *too* much. (*She moves to* L *of Penelope*)

PENELOPE. *Much* too much.

MISS SKILLON. You have deliberately robbed me of my right-hand man.

PENELOPE (*in a sudden burst of irritation*) Well, good heavens, you can use your *left*, can't you?

MISS SKILLON (*speechless*) I—I . . .

PENELOPE (*calmly*) And Miss Skillon, I really must ask you to get all your—(*with a wave of the hand*) paraphernalia out of here.

MISS SKILLON. Para . . . !

PENELOPE (*moving to the map on the floor*) I'm expecting—a visitor at any moment. I cannot have the place looking like Epsom after Derby Day.

MISS SKILLON. I must have a headquarters to work from. This search for your husband may take hours.

PENELOPE (*scooping the box and flags on to the map and placing it in Miss Skillon's arms; not aggressively*) The potting shed is at your disposal.

MISS SKILLON (*fuming*) You haven't heard the last of this, Mrs Toop. Such callousness. (*She moves to the french windows*)

PENELOPE (*quite pleasantly*) If you find it cold, there's a stove under the bench. (*She propels Miss Skillon gently but firmly out of the french windows*)

(MISS SKILLON *exits by the french windows*)

(*She turns and moves* C, *runs her hand over her head, thinking, then remembers something. Almost brightly*) Oh, yes. (*She picks up the tray with the coffee, looks cautiously towards the french windows, then goes to the cupboard door and knocks on it*)

LIONEL (*in the cupboard*) Go away. I'm out.

PENELOPE. Don't be silly; it's me.

(LIONEL *emerges from the cupboard and moves down* L)

LIONEL. I thought you were Miss Skillon. She's locked up my wardrobe and taken the key.

PENELOPE (*looking at Lionel's tartan rug*) Lionel! So that's what you're up to. You're leaving me.

LIONEL. Leaving me? (*He crosses to* R)

PENELOPE (*following Lionel and pointing to the rug*) You're joining the Gordon Highlanders. Darling, you mustn't. You haven't the right kind of knees.

(PENELOPE *chases* LIONEL *round the right end of the sofa and up* C *and tries to lift his "kilt"*)

LIONEL. This is no time for horseplay.

PENELOPE. Well, I want to see if it's true.

LIONEL. Where is Miss Skillon?

PENELOPE. I've put her in the potting shed, you can relax.

LIONEL. Are you sure?

PENELOPE. Positive.

LIONEL (*crossing to the fire*) I find it chilly in that cupboard.

PENELOPE. I'm not surprised. I've brought you some coffee.
LIONEL. I need something stronger than coffee.
PENELOPE. Lionel!
LIONEL. Well, you know what the doctor said about my blood-pressure, it's low.

(PENELOPE *puts the tray on the sideboard* L, *takes out a bottle and two glasses from the sideboard and pours two drinks*)

PENELOPE. I'll get you a glass of elderberry wine—that'll push it up. I was saving this for Christmas—to pour over Miss Skillon and set her alight.
LIONEL (*sitting on the sofa*) I never thought the day would come when I'd skulk in the cupboard of my own home.
PENELOPE (*crossing and standing behind the sofa*) Never mind, put your feet up.

(LIONEL *puts his feet up*)

Not too far up. (*She hands him a glass of wine*) Bottoms up!
LIONEL. Penelope, this isn't a cocktail party—this is just what the doctor ordered.
PENELOPE. I know, I made it.
LIONEL. Humphrey in church?
PENELOPE. Yes.
LIONEL. I hope he isn't the only one.
PENELOPE (*crossing to* L) Now, darling, you mustn't be discouraged. I know business is bad.
LIONEL. Business? Penelope, really!
PENELOPE. But it might pick up. We must hold our heads high and cling to our faith in the Pools—er—Heaven.
LIONEL. I wish Heaven would send me some trousers. I'm sorry, I shouldn't have said that.
PENELOPE (*moving to* L *of the sofa*) Lionel, suppose Heaven were to grant you every one of your wishes and me every one of mine.
LIONEL. You mean . . . ?
PENELOPE (*moving behind the sofa*) I mean, suppose Heaven paid the electric light bill and all the other bills and paid for a new coat of paint all over the Vicarage and, let me see, what else?
LIONEL. Some new bells for my church?
PENELOPE. Dozens of 'em, all shapes and sizes. And new hassocks; so that people can pray without breaking their kneecaps. An oven that does its own cooking—a bottle of French perfume—"My Sin". Economy size. (*She crosses to* L *of the armchair*) A washing machine—and something I've always wanted . . .
LIONEL. What's that?
PENELOPE (*crossing to the sofa*) A mink bedspread.
LIONEL. I say, steady.
PENELOPE (*sitting on the left arm of the sofa*) A new car for you, with safety belts. Oh, and I just don't know. Lionel, suppose Heaven sent you all these things—what would you say?
LIONEL. Say? "Thank you very much."

PENELOPE. Would you take them?
LIONEL. Take them? Of course I'd take them.
PENELOPE (*rising*) *Lionel!*
LIONEL. If Heaven sent them.
PENELOPE (*resuming her seat*) But Heaven sometimes appears in strange forms. Look at manna.
LIONEL. Manna?
PENELOPE. From Heaven. It fell all over the Israelites—you remember. And they all got turned into pillars of salt.
LIONEL. Penelope, there are certain inaccuracies in your Biblical observations.
PENELOPE. All I'm saying is, you never know which way Heaven is going to jump.
LIONEL. Jump?
PENELOPE. You didn't know Miss Skillon was going to put you to bed, did you?
LIONEL. That wasn't Heaven, that was . . .
PENELOPE. Lionel! And now out of the blue, uncle is coming to lunch.
LIONEL (*rising*) The Bishop? He mustn't see me like this. Penelope, you must find me some trousers.
PENELOPE (*rising and crossing to* L) Well, you're not having mine.
LIONEL. That's another thing—Penelope, you know how I disapprove of your wearing garments normally worn by members of the opposite sex.

(PENELOPE *reacts to Lionel's "kilt"*)

I don't like you in trousers, I wish you'd take them off.
PENELOPE (*starting to unzip*) Oh, all right, then.
LIONEL. No, no, you mustn't do it here.

(HUMPHREY *enters by the french windows. He is in cassock and surplice*)

(*To Humphrey*) Anything wrong?
HUMPHREY. Mr Toop, it's the church. There's no-one in it.
PENELOPE. No?
HUMPHREY. No choir, no congregation, not a soul to be saved—er—seen.
PENELOPE (*crossing to* C) Empty houses, Mr Humphrey—I know. I've played Oldham. But not to worry. And if you don't mind my saying it, how very nice you look.
HUMPHREY. Nice?
PENELOPE. Your cassock and surplice. So nice.
HUMPHREY. How nice!
PENELOPE. And however do you . . . ? It's amazing!
HUMPHREY. What is?
PENELOPE. Your surplice, so white. And not just white, but shining, shining white. (*She puts her glass on the coffee tray, picks up the tray, moves to the kitchen door and turns*) When a mother cares, it shows.

(PENELOPE *exits to the kitchen.* HUMPHREY *sits in the armchair*)

LIONEL (*crossing to the sideboard*) I'm sorry about the house—er—church. (*He puts his glass on the sideboard then crosses to* C) How are attendances at Badcaster?

HUMPHREY. Sometimes I outnumber them there, too.

LIONEL. I suppose the answer rests with us, Humphrey. Do we lack something today?

(HUMPHREY *glances at where Lionel's trousers should be*)

I wonder if there's an old pair in the attic. (*He moves to the stairs*) I'll go and rummage around if you'll forgive me. (*He goes up the stairs*) Help yourself to a book if you'd care to. Something rather distinguished about a kilt—I wouldn't mind the privilege of wearing the tartan myself. I wonder if there's a clan MacToop?

(LIONEL *exits at the top of the stairs.* HUMPHREY *rises, moves up* C *and holds the front of his surplice up to the light.*

IDA *enters by the french windows. She carries a tin of corned beef and a copy of the "News of the World"*)

IDA (*as she enters*) Please'm . . . (*She sees Humphrey*) Aah! Oh, my goodness!

(HUMPHREY *spins round to the armchair*)

Oh, Mr Humphrey. It's only you. (*She pants breathlessly*) Mr Humphrey, are you any good with bicycles?

HUMPHREY (*weakly*) Bicycles?

IDA. Mending 'em, I mean. (*Breathlessly*) You see—Miss Skillon wouldn't lend me hers, so I borrowed it. (*She points out of the french windows*) It's just outside and the chain's broke. And if Miss Skillon sees it . . .

HUMPHREY (*dazed*) But I'm not very good with hammer and nails.

IDA (*eagerly*) Oh, you don't have to be very good—just so long as you mend it. (*She moves to the kitchen door*) I've got to take this—(*she holds up the tin of corned beef*) to Mrs Toop. She's very worried. There isn't much of it, is there? But it's all mother had.

(HUMPHREY'S *head is swimming*)

(*Pleadingly*) Mr Humphrey—to help Mrs Toop out—at lunch—when she offers you some corned beef—will you just say "No, thank you, I'm not hungry"?

(IDA *exits to the kitchen.* HUMPHREY, *in anguish, rotates in his tracks then collapses on to the sofa*)

HUMPHREY. Shining white beef? (*With a sob in his voice*) They're mad! Insane! They should be put away—all of them. (*In his distress he beats the sofa seat*)

(LIONEL *enters down the stairs*)

Lionel (*cautiously*) Sssssss! Ssss!

(Humphrey *sits up, startled*)

(*A little louder*) Sssssss!

(Humphrey *looks around on the floor trying to locate the sound. He does not see Lionel*)

(*Longer and louder*) Sssssssssss!

Humphrey (*wretchedly*) Oh, *no!* Not *snakes* as well. (*He lifts his feet on to the sofa*)

(Lionel *crosses to* L *of the sofa*)

Lionel. Don't be silly, it's only me. You haven't got a spare pair of trousers, I suppose? No, of course you haven't—I'll take another look in the cupboard.

(Lionel *crosses, goes into the cupboard and closes the door.* Ida *bursts in from the kitchen, carrying the newspaper*)

Ida (*as she enters; as if she had never left the room*) Oh, and Mr Humphrey . . .

Humphrey (*leaping up; with a wild, terrified cry*) *No!*

Ida (*crossing to* L *of Humphrey; with very mild surprise*) Oooh! *Aren't* you a nervous kitten. You ought to take something.

(Humphrey *collapses on to the sofa and puts his feet up*)

Look. (*She holds out the newspaper*) I quite forgot. I brought you this

Humphrey. What?

Ida. The *News of the World*—remember? You said you wanted it. It's mother's copy, really, but I told her how lost you were without it, so she said, "Let the poor little devil have it." (*She puts the paper on Humphrey's lap*) There! Now you just put your feet up.

Humphrey. They are up.

Ida (*crossing to the kitchen door*) Why shouldn't you? (*She stops and turns*) Oh, and I've told Mrs Toop what you're going to say at lunch. She's ever so grateful.

(Ida *exits to the kitchen.* Humphrey *reacts, and shakes his head as if trying to rid it of its throbbing. He then automatically lifts the paper from his knee. Without unfolding it, he gazes at it absently for a moment, then gives a start of remembrance*)

Humphrey. Oh. My form. (*He pats his chest as if tapping his pocket*) Where did I put . . . ? (*He remembers*) Oh, yes, of course. (*He rises, gives a quick, guilty look around the room, then searches eagerly under the sofa cushion, but does not find the coupon*) Amazing! I'm sure I . . . *I know* I . . . (*He goes on to his knees, gropes under the sofa and searches around the carpet, his back to the kitchen door and bent well down*)

(Penelope *enters from the kitchen*)

(*He finds Willie's coupon under the edge of the carpet*) Ah!

(PENELOPE, *seeing Humphrey on his knees and misconstruing the reason, goes half-way up the stairs, then stops and turns*)

PENELOPE. Say a little one for me.

(PENELOPE *exits at the top of the stairs.* HUMPHREY, *still on hands and knees, motionless, watches her go. He holds this position for a moment then rises and sits on the sofa*)

HUMPHREY (*somewhat breathlessly*) Ah! I *knew* I . . . (*He smoothes out the form, opens the newspaper, finds the necessary page and lays the paper across his knee. He puts the coupon* R *of him on the sofa seat and while checking, his head is contantly turning, with a little jerk from coupon to paper and paper to coupon. This happens almost like clockwork. As he checks he murmurs the names of the teams*) Arsenal—Wolves; Chelsea—Sheffield Wednesday; Luton—Liverpool; Cardiff—Preston North End . . .

(LIONEL *emerges from the cupboard wearing gum-boots and a large surplice. He looks out of the french windows, opens the kitchen door, peers out, closes the door then begins to creep up the stairs. He becomes aware of Humphrey and stops*)

LIONEL. Mr Humphrey! Are you all right? (*He comes down the stairs and crosses to Humphrey*)

(HUMPHREY *rises, picks up the coupon, leaves the newspaper on the left end of the sofa and crosses to* C)

HUMPHREY (*excitedly*) Oh, Mr Toop, such news, such wonderful news. Oh, happy Humphrey! I want to dance. I want to sing. (*He sings*)

"All things bright and beautiful,
All creatures great and small . . ."

LIONEL (*aghast*) Mr Humphrey, have you been drinking?

HUMPHREY. No—not yet. (*He seizes Lionel and twirls him round*) Tra-la-la-la. Hey diddle diddle!

LIONEL. *Mr Humphrey!*

(*They stand* C. HUMPHREY *is* L *of Lionel*)

HUMPHREY (*holding the coupon behind his back*) Mr Toop, Mr Toop, I think it's happened.

LIONEL. What has?

HUMPHREY. My treble chance. I think it's coming up.

LIONEL. Then shouldn't you wear a belt or something?

HUMPHREY. No, no! My Pool.

LIONEL. Your what?

HUMPHREY. My Pool—football, you know. (*To demonstrate, he quickly lifts his cassock a fraction and gives a little kick, catching Lionel on his bad leg*)

LIONEL (*with a howl*) Dur!

HUMPHREY (*putting the coupon on the table* C) Oh, Mr Toop, I'm so sorry. I got carried away. Did it hurt?

LIONEL (*yelling*) Yes! (*He crosses to the sofa*)

HUMPHREY. Let me assist you.

LIONEL (*lying on the sofa*) Assist me! Don't dare to touch me! You gambler!

HUMPHREY (*sitting* L *of Lionel on the sofa and putting his hands on Lionel's legs*) Mr Toop!

LIONEL. Take your hands off my Wellingtons, Mr Humphrey. Shame on you! I can't believe my ears.

HUMPHREY. Oh, but you must; that is, if I can believe my eyes.

LIONEL. That you—at your age and in your cloth—should gamble in a Pool. Oh, Humphrey—Humphrey!

HUMPHREY. Oh, Toopy—Toopy! (*He blows his nose*)

LIONEL (*rising, crossing above the sofa to* L *of it and facing Humphrey*) You must leave my house.

HUMPHREY (*pleading*) No.

LIONEL. Taking with you your ill-gotten gains.

HUMPHREY. But I haven't got them yet.

LIONEL. Leaving me secure in the knowledge that I do not share your craving for wealth. (*He turns his back to Humphrey*) That I am content with my own little lot.

HUMPHREY. I haven't even got a little lot. (*He kneels up on the sofa and places his hands on Lionel's shoulder. Pleading*) Mr Toop, let me explain. How little you know Arthur Humphrey.

LIONEL. I intend to know him even less. (*He crosses to* C)

(HUMPHREY, *losing his grip on Lionel's shoulders, automatically loses his balance. He begins to fall over the left end of the sofa but just manages to save himself from going right over*)

HUMPHREY. Oh, my goodness! (*He struggles upright*) Not one penny of what I haven't yet got will go into my own pocket.

LIONEL. Ha! (*He crosses above the sofa and goes down* R)

(HUMPHREY *moves to get off the sofa and follow Lionel, but his feet are now entangled with his cassock. He struggles to free them*)

HUMPHREY. I'll be with you in a minute. (*He struggles*) I seem to have lost my feet. (*He struggles and his feet emerge. He points to his feet*) Ah! There they are. (*He rises and stands below the sofa*) Mr Toop, have you ever been troubled by the death—watch beetle?

LIONEL. I can't say I have.

HUMPHREY. It's all over the roof of my church—bleeding it . . .

LIONEL. What?

HUMPHREY. I must stop the bleeder. (*He sits on the sofa*)

LIONEL. *What?* (*He sits* R *of Humphrey on the sofa*)

HUMPHREY. During service, little bits of plaster descend on my congregation. It gets in their hair.

LIONEL. It would get in mine.

HUMPHREY. One hardly dare pray for a sight of Heaven, in case the ceiling comes down and they get it.

LIONEL. You must do something about it. You must take steps.

HUMPHREY. I did! I did! I started a fund. In three months all I got was two two-shilling pieces–and one of those was bad.

Lionel. Ah! That rings a bell—or rather, it doesn't.
Humphrey. What does?
Lionel. Have you ever been troubled by bells?
Humphrey. Bells?
Lionel. I want new bells in my belfry. I started a fund. I told my congregation "Stop at nothing"—and they did.
Humphrey. Then we're both in the same boat. Now, here comes my point, Mr Toop. Hearing of fortunes won on the Pools, I began to dabble.
Lionel. Dabble?
Humphrey. I dabbled and dabbled. Can you blame me, Mr Toop?
Lionel. You mean you dabbled, not for yourself, but for your beetles?
Humphrey. Yes. There's no harm in that, is there?
Lionel. Er—no—I suppose—er . . .
Humphrey (*rising and crossing to* c) And now, if my forecast is correct, I have succeeded beyond my wildest dreams. I shall have enough and to spare.
Lionel. To spare?
Humphrey. For other worthy causes.
Lionel. My bells! (*He rises and crosses to* r *of Humphrey*) Mr Humphrey—I accept your offer.
Humphrey. Have I made an offer? Oh, I see—a take-over bid.
Lionel. Do you mind?
Humphrey. Not at all.
Lionel. Not one penny for our own uses.
Humphrey. No, of course not. Though I have thought that perhaps a motor scooter would be nice.
Lionel. A motor scooter?
Humphrey. To get around the parish.
Lionel. A motor scooter—to get around the . . . Indeed, why not? (*Excitedly*) Now, what do you mean, if your forecast is correct? Don't you know?
Humphrey (*excitedly*) Well, of course, I—I—only checked it *once*, and—my reading glasses—I left them in the vestry.
Lionel (*impatiently*) We must check again.
Humphrey (*blinking*) "We"?
Lionel. At once. How do we do it?
Humphrey (*leaping into action*) The paper. (*He points to the sofa*) The *News of the World.*

(Lionel *picks up the newspaper and glances at it*)

Lionel (*reading*) "Archdeacon tells all!" Oh, surely not!
Humphrey (*looking around*) And the form? Oh, my goodness! Where did I . . . ? (*He crosses and searches frantically on the sofa*)
Lionel. What does it look like?

(Humphrey *straightens up, looks* l *and sees the coupon on the table* lc)

Humphrey. Ah! There it is. (*He crosses to the table* lc)

(*The front-door bell rings.* HUMPHREY *has his hand outstretched to pick up the coupon when* MISS SKILLON'S *voice is heard off in the garden*)

MISS SKILLON (*off*) Who has done this? Mrs Toop . . .

(LIONEL *grabs* HUMPHREY *by the arm and drags him towards the cupboard*)

LIONEL. Mr Humphrey! Hurry! Miss Skillon!

HUMPHREY (*as he is dragged to the cupboard*) But, Mr Toop! The form—to check . . . (*He waves the newspaper towards the coupon on the table* LC)

(LIONEL *pushes* HUMPHREY *into the cupboard, follows him in and quickly closes the door*)

MISS SKILLON (*off*) Someone shall pay for this.

(*The* BISHOP OF LAX *enters from the hall. He is a large, quite amiable, but dignified man. He wears bishop's garb, including gaiters. He is wearing his hat, not a tophat, but a large black Homburg with the traditional bishop's rosette in front. He carries a bag and coat. He removes his hat and puts it on the table* LC, *covering the Pools coupon. He stands quite still, facing* L, *then looks around, moving his head only. After a while he calls in a low voice*)

BISHOP. Toop! Toop!

(MISS SKILLON *enters by the french windows, wheeling a very old and shabby bicycle. She wheels the bicycle just behind the Bishop, stops and rings the bell*)

(*He turns, startled, but moves aside with great dignity*) I'm *so* sorry.

(MISS SKILLON *wheels the bicycle off into the hall*)

(*He looks after Miss Skillon, his face "dead-pan", then puts his bag and coat on the chair up* LC, *moves* C *and looks around, a little "lost" but not unduly perturbed. After a few moments he clears his throat, pauses, then moves to the french windows, looks out then moves down* L) Nice *garden!* (*He looks into the hall*)

(*The cupboard door opens cautiously.*

HUMPHREY, *after a quick, cursory look, begins to emerge. He is almost out of the cupboard when he sees the Bishop's back*)

HUMPHREY (*startled*) Oh, my . . . !

(HUMPHREY *quickly steps back into the cupboard and closes the door with a little slam. The* BISHOP *spins round, but too late. He again stands quite still, puzzled but dignified. After a pause, his eye happens to catch the window*)

BISHOP (*quietly*) *Very* nice garden. (*He crosses to the fireplace, sees the nude statuette on the mantelpiece and reacts. He hums quietly to himself, his choice being "Lead Kindly Light". He takes a book from the mantelpiece and opens it*)

"Lead kindly light
Amid the encircling gloom,
Lead thou me on . . ."

HUMPHREY (*in the cupboard; singing*)

"The night is dark
And I am far from home,
Lead thou me on . . ."

LIONEL (*in the cupboard*) Ssh!

(*The* BISHOP *reacts. After Humphrey has finished singing, the* BISHOP *looks around, puzzled, and replaces the book on the mantelpiece*)

BISHOP (*calling*) Any . . . (*There is a slight "frog" in his throat. He clears it and starts again*) Anyone at home?

(*There is a silence.*
WILLIE, *still in cassock and surplice, enters by the french windows. There is a look of misery and bewilderment on his face as he moves slowly down* L, *his eyes glued on Humphrey's Pools coupon he holds in both hands. He ignores the Bishop. He puts the coupon on the table* LC, *and gazes at it. The* BISHOP, *his face "dead-pan" watches Willie*)

WILLIE (*wretchedly; in a just audible mutter*) Arsenal—Wolves . . . I could've swore . . .

(*The* BISHOP *crosses to* C)

BISHOP (*dignified, but with a little uncertainty in his voice*) Er—*good* morning.

(WILLIE *turns and looks at the Bishop, his face expressing neither surprise nor interest*)

WILLIE (*gloomily*) *Ar!* I could've swore I gave 'em all draws.

(WILLIE *leaves the coupon on the table* LC *and exits slowly to the hall*)

BISHOP (*puzzled*) Draws? (*He sees the spinning-wheel down* L) Ah, a spinning-wheel, how quaint. (*He moves to the oak chair down* L, *sits beside the spinning-wheel, reacts to the hard seat, rises, collects the cushion from the armchair, puts it on the chair down* L, *sits and turns the spinning-wheel, singing very quietly*) "When a maiden loves, she sits and sighs . . ." (*He remembers himself, then sits quite still for a moment or two, very conscious of the fact that he is being neglected. He rises, crosses to the desk, picks up the "Church Times" and stands with his back to the room*)

(*As he does so, the cupboard door opens.*
LIONEL *emerges from the cupboard, tiptoes to the chair down* L *and picks up the cushion*)

(*He calls*) Toop! Toop!
LIONEL (*unconsciously*) Yes?

(LIONEL *reacts and darts back into the cupboard with the cushion, closing the door behind him. The* BISHOP *reacts to the "Yes?" without turn-*

ing. When LIONEL *is in the cupboard, the* BISHOP *turns and looks around the room, puzzled. He crosses with the "Church Times" to the chair down* L, *sits, then reacts on finding the seat hard. He rises, looks blankly at the seat of the chair, then under and around it, then, more puzzled than ever, sits.*

IDA *dashes in from the hall. Completely ignoring the Bishop, she runs to the kitchen door*)

IDA (*wildly*) Willie, Willie! You mustn't do it. *Willie!*

(IDA *exits to the kitchen. The* BISHOP *reacts, then after a moment, rises, crosses and drops the "Church Times" on the sofa, goes to the desk and is about to sit at it.*

MISS SKILLON *enters from the hall, crosses to the french windows, puts her finger in her mouth and loudly "yoo-hoos". The* BISHOP *jumps and turns*

MISS SKILLON *exits by the french windows. The* BISHOP *stands for a moment then sits at the desk, draws a sheet of notepaper from the rack and takes up a pen*)

BISHOP (*writing; in a nearly matter-of-fact voice*) "My dear—Penelope . . ." (*He stops and sits thinking, his pen tapping the desk*)

(*The cupboard door opens.*

HUMPHREY *emerges from the cupboard on hands and knees and creeps slowly towards the table* LC. *He gets into a position* L *of the table so that his body is hidden from the audience by the armchair, and from the Bishop by the table. His hand rises over the table-top and begins exploring it. The* BISHOP, *sitting with his back to the table, becomes "aware" of something "happening". Still seated, he turns and sees the exploring hand. He gives no violent start, but just watches the hand for a moment, his face "dead-pan". He then looks out front, very faintly puzzled.*

HUMPHREY'S *hand finds the coupon deposited by Willie. He takes the coupon, crawls quickly into the cupboard and closes the door. The* BISHOP *turns, rises, and very dignified, crosses to the table* LC. *He looks at it and under it, then, after a moment, and still "dead-pan" he returns to the desk, sits and resumes writing*)

(*As he writes. Calmly*) "Sorry my visit has been of so—*short* duration—especially after the—*cordiality* of my reception." (*He writes a little more, fairly quickly, and merely mumbles until he comes to the climax, which he speaks*) ". . . you a—*Merry Christmas.* Your devoted—but baffled uncle." (*He quite quickly puts the note in an envelope, seals it, writes "Penelope" on it, rises, places it on the mantelpiece then crosses to the table* LC *and picks up his hat, revealing, but ignoring, the other coupon. He puts his hat on*)

(PENELOPE *enters down the stairs, sees the Bishop, gives a little "Aw", turns and goes up the stairs*)

(*He turns and watches Penelope until she is nearly at the top of the stairs*) Penelope! Is that you?

PENELOPE (*stopping and turning; surprised and "caught on the hop"*) *Uncle!* (*She runs down the stairs*) It *is* nice to see you.

BISHOP. Penelope!

(*They embrace*)

PENELOPE. *Darling!* (*She gives him another little hug*) Do you like corned beef?
BISHOP (*after the slightest pause*) I loathe it.
PENELOPE (*flatly*) Oh. (*She moves down* C. *Brightly*) Oh, well! Why didn't anyone tell me you were here?
BISHOP (*moving to* L *of Penelope*) I don't think anyone cared. I—I rang the bell.
PENELOPE. Ah, that explains it. It doesn't always work.
BISHOP (*gravely*) I see. But the front door was open so I came in.
PENELOPE. How wise of you.
BISHOP. I wonder.
PENELOPE (*looking at his hat*) Oh, darling! (*With disapproval*) That hat! Where's your nice topper?
BISHOP (*removing his hat; solemnly*) The Dean sat on it last week, and I can't afford another.
PENELOPE (*taking the hat*) Well—er . . . (*She puts the hat on the table* LC, *but does not cover the coupon*) Come and sit down, Uncle. (*She crosses to the fireplace*)
BISHOP (*watching Penelope closely*) Thank you.
PENELOPE. You must forgive me if I seem a little—distrait, but . . .

(*The* BISHOP *crosses to the sofa*)

(*She sees the envelope on the mantelpiece, picks it up and looks at it*) Oh. (*She holds it up apologetically*) Excuse me. (*She opens the envelope*)

(IDA *hurries in from the kitchen*)

IDA (*as she enters*) Please'm . . . (*She is rushing across to Penelope when she becomes aware of the Bishop, stops, drops a full curtsy and murmurs with awe*) Your Grace! (*She rises and crosses to Penelope*) Please'm . . .

(*The* BISHOP *subsides on to the sofa*)

PENELOPE (*automatically taking the note out of the envelope*) What is it, Ida? (*She glances at the note without really taking in the contents*)
IDA (*urgently*) Will you come and see Willie'm?
PENELOPE. Willie? But I can't just now—not with . . . (*She indicates the Bishop*)
IDA. He's in a terrible state'm.
PENELOPE. Why—what . . . ?
IDA (*more urgently*) He says . . . (*To the Bishop*) This isn't for your ears, Your Grace. (*To Penelope*) If his Pools don't come out he's going to . . . (*She whispers in Penelope's ear*)

(*The* BISHOP *looks out front*)

PENELOPE (*with dismay and horror*) Oh—no!
IDA (*vigorously nodding her head*) Yes'm!
PENELOPE. Oh—Ida!
IDA. Oh—mum! (*She gives a sniff, suggesting tears*)

PENELOPE (*automatically looking at the note*) Where is Willie?

IDA. In the kitchen'm—if he isn't in the pond by now.

PENELOPE. I'll come right away.

IDA (*fervently*) Thank you'm. (*She is dashing to the kitchen door when she remembers, turns, pulls herself together, gives a low curtsy to the Bishop and murmurs*) Your Grace!

(IDA *exits quickly to the kitchen*)

PENELOPE (*obviously upset; still giving half-hearted glances at the note*) Uncle, would you forgive me for a moment, if I—er . . . (*She glances at the note*) Oh, *isn't* that nice! (*She hands the note to the Bishop*) Look, darling. He wishes me a Merry Christmas.

(PENELOPE *crosses and exits to the kitchen. The* BISHOP, *completely "dead-pan", sits with the note in his hand, looking out front. His left hand beats a slow tattoo on his knee. After a moment or two, he rises, moves unhurriedly to the desk, drops the note in the waste-paper basket, sits at the desk and very deliberately begins to write*)

BISHOP (*as he writes; with the faintest suggestion of an edge to his voice*) "My—dear—Penelope . . ."

(*There comes a heartbroken cry from the cupboard*)

HUMPHREY (*in the cupboard*) No! *No!*

(*The* BISHOP'S *head comes up slowly. He lays the pen down and, still seated, slowly turns and looks towards the cupboard*)

(*Quieter, but more agonized*) No-o-o!

(*The* BISHOP *slowly turns and looks out front, "dead-pan". He then quite unhurriedly, rises, and equally unhurriedly, crosses to the cupboard and after a moment's pause he opens the cupboard door quite normally and stands well to one side so that the interior of the cupboard is seen. The cupboard light is on.* LIONEL *and* HUMPHREY *are seated on a laundry basket, just inside the door.* LIONEL *is reading from the "News of the World" and* HUMPHREY *is checking the coupon. They are too engrossed to notice the Bishop*)

LIONEL (*in a flat, but deliberate voice*) Everton, *four*; Manchester United, *two*.

(*The* BISHOP, *horrified, closes the door. He stands in front of it for a moment or two, "dead-pan", then crosses unhurriedly to the desk, takes up his second note, tears it across and drops it in the waste-paper basket. He crosses to the table* LC, *picks up his hat and moves towards the french windows.*

IDA *and* WILLIE *enter by the french windows.* IDA *is almost pulling Willie into the room. She is very agitated*)

IDA (*as she enters*) No, Willie, *no!* You mustn't do it; you *mustn't.* (*She sees the Bishop and drags Willie to him. Without preamble*) Your Grace, tell him he mustn't do it.

BISHOP (*after the slightest pause*) You mustn't do it, my boy,

IDA (*to Willie*) You see! The *Bishop*—the Church's *one* foundation—says you mustn't do it.

WILLIE (*calmly*) But I . . .

(PENELOPE *hurries in from the hall*)

IDA (*indicating Willie; eagerly*) Look'm! I caught him.

PENELOPE (*crossing to Ida and Willie*) Oh, thank heaven! Willie—you had us scared.

IDA. When I looked out of the kitchen window'm, and saw him walking to oblivion . . .

WILLIE (*practically*) I was walking to the *vestry*.

(*The* BISHOP *crosses to the fireplace*)

PENELOPE. What?

WILLIE. Ar! To get shot of these. (*He gives his surplice a little tug*)

IDA (*indignantly*) You mean you weren't going to do away with yourself? And I told Mrs Toop I was *sure* you . . . Willie Briggs, I'll never forgive you.

PENELOPE (*severely at first*) And I'll never forgive you, Ida, scaring us all like that.

(PENELOPE *turns to include the* BISHOP *in the "all" with a smile, then becomes conscious of his immobility, his detachment, and his "dead-pan" face*)

IDA (*to Willie*) And I'll never forgive you, neither, for raising our hopes the way you did.

(PENELOPE *takes a step towards the Bishop*)

PENELOPE (*to the Bishop; rather strained*) Cup of tea, Uncle?

BISHOP (*politely*) No, thank you. (*He puts his hat over the statuette*)

IDA (*to Willie*) Making out we'd won a fortune when we 'adn't.

PENELOPE (*to the Bishop*) Coffee?

(*The* BISHOP *merely turns his "dead-pan" gaze on Penelope*)

IDA (*still attacking Willie*) You should've made certain before you ever told us. (*To Penelope*) *Shouldn't* he, 'm?

PENELOPE (*still coping with the Bishop; more strained*) We—er—we thought lunch about—(*she consults her wrist watch*) one?

BISHOP (*quietly*) I think your—(*with the slightest of gestures towards Ida*) *corroboration* is required.

PENELOPE (*somewhat dizzily*) What? Oh! (*She turns to Ida*) Ida, what is it you . . . ?

IDA. I was saying'm—Willie should have made certain before he . . .

WILLIE (*desperately*) I *was* certain, practically. (*He moves to the table* LC) I'm *sure* I 'ad it right.

IDA (*following Willie*) How can it be right when you say it's wrong.

(WILLIE *dejectedly picks up the coupon from the table*)

(*Insistently*) *Is* it wrong?

WILLIE (*not really looking at the coupon*) Ar! (*He sits in the armchair*)

IDA (*almost impatiently*) Then if it's *wrong* it can't be *right*, can it? (*She turns to the Bishop*) Even you can see that, can't you, Your Grace?

(*The* BISHOP *refuses to be drawn. There is an awkward pause*)

PENELOPE (*crossing to the Bishop*) It's wonderful seeing you again, Uncle, but of course, if only I'd known a little earlier . . .

(*Another heartrending cry comes from the cupboard*)

HUMPHREY (*in the cupboard*) No—*no!*

(*The heads of* PENELOPE, IDA *and* WILLIE *come up with a jerk. Their faces express horror and bewilderment. The* BISHOP'S *face expresses nothing. After a moment,* PENELOPE *looks apprehensively at the Bishop.* WILLIE *studies the coupon*)

BISHOP (*turning his "dead-pan" gaze on Penelope*) You were saying . . . ?

PENELOPE. I—I've forgotten—somehow.

(*There is a strained silence for a moment, then* WILLIE *gives a sudden, sharp cry of incredulity and horror*)

WILLIE (*gaping at the coupon*) Aah!

(PENELOPE, *whose nerves are stretched to breaking point, almost leaps into the air*)

PENELOPE. Aaaah! (*She recovers. Almost angrily*) Willie, don't do that again. (*In a somewhat calmer voice*) The Bishop's nerves can't stand it.

WILLIE (*gaping at the coupon*) It *is* right!

IDA. *What?*

WILLIE. My Pools. (*He rises and moves down* L) It's right, I tell you.

IDA. Oh, *Willie* . . .

WILLIE (*desperately*) If it isn't—then I'm going up the wall.

IDA (*firmly*) No, you're not. These walls have just been cleaned down.

WILLIE. Mrs Toop! Mrs Toop! Look! I'm sure—(*he pulls his newspaper from his pocket*) come and look, Mrs Toop.

PENELOPE (*after a moment's hesitation; to the Bishop*) Excuse me. (*She crosses quickly to Willie*)

WILLIE (*mystified*) I don't understand it, mum. One time it's wrong, and the next it's . . .

IDA (*moving* C; *sharply*) Don't say it's right till you're *certain* this time.

WILLIE (*desperately*) Look'm, will you check *with* me?

PENELOPE (*dizzily*) What? But, Willie, I don't understand it. It's all double-Dutch to me.

WILLIE (*handing the newspaper to Penelope*) Well, you see. All you've got to do, *see*, is . . .

PENELOPE (*gaping at the paper*) No, Willie, I'm afraid I don't see. I'm sorry to be so stupid.

IDA (*almost whimpering in her agitation*) Oh, dear! (*She looks desperately around and her eyes fall on the Bishop*)

(*The* BISHOP, *who has not moved an inch, is watching the proceedings, his face a blank*)

(*With relief*) Ah! (*She takes the paper from Penelope*) 'Scuse me. (*She crosses to the Bishop and curtsies*) Your Grace—(*pleadingly*) you're used to *reading*. Would you . . . ?

PENELOPE (*quickly*) No, no, Ida. We can't ask Uncle to . . .

IDA (*looking sadly at Penelope*) Why not'm?

PENELOPE. Good heavens, no! After all, Uncle *is* a bishop.

(IDA *addresses the Bishop innocently and inoffensively*)

IDA. Yes, but—(*she looks the Bishop wistfully up and down*) I'm sure he's not as black as he's painted. Your Grace—(*with a half curtsy*) you will, won't you? (*With a winning smile*) Just to please Ida.

(*The* BISHOP *remains unflinching and completely "dead-pan"*)

BISHOP (*taking the paper from Ida*) What exactly do I . . . ?

IDA (*clapping her hands in delight*) He's going to do it. I knew he would. (*She is about to put her hands on the Bishop's arm, but stops just in time*) You *are* wonderful!

BISHOP. Thank you. But would you mind telling me exactly what I . . .

IDA (*taking charge*) Well, first of all you sit down. (*She rushes behind the sofa, leans over the back, plumps up the cushions, puts one* C *as a back-rest for the Bishop and pats it*) Here, if it's all the same to you.

(*The* BISHOP, *after a look at Penelope, sits* C *of the sofa, very dignified and very upright*)

(*Happily*) That's right. (*She moves down* L *of the sofa, turns and smiles at the Bishop*) You can relax if you want to. (*To Willie*) Now, Willlie, you sit next to His Grace—(*she points to* R *of the Bishop*) over there.

(WILLIE *crosses and sits gingerly* R *of the Bishop on the sofa*)

(*Happily*) There! That's *you* two settled. And I'll sit here. (*She sits* L *of the Bishop on the sofa, cosily tucking her legs under her*)

(*The* BISHOP'S *gaze turns on Ida for a second*)

For *luck*.

(*The* BISHOP *looks out front*)

(*She looks at Penelope*) Oh! What about you'm?

(IDA *wriggles round to look at Penelope, thus causing the* BISHOP *a little discomfort for a moment.* PENELOPE, *who can hardly believe all this is happening, and is expecting the Bishop to explode at any moment, moves and sits on the back of the sofa*)

PENELOPE (*dazed*) I'm all right here.
IDA (*enthusiastically*) *That's* all right, then. (*She wriggles back into her original position*)

(*The* BISHOP *is again joggled slightly, but remains "dead-pan" while adjusting himself*)

(*She looks quickly at Willie, the Bishop and Penelope. Happily*) We ought to have our photos took.
BISHOP (*indicating the paper; quietly*) *Shall* we—er . . .
IDA (*misunderstanding*) Oh, no! There isn't time. 'Sides, we haven't got a camera.

(*The* BISHOP'S *eyes close.* WILLIE *gives the Bishop a gentle prod. The* BISHOP *opens his eyes and looks at Willie*)

WILLIE. You ever 'ad a parrot?
BISHOP. Never.
WILLIE. That's what I'm goin' to 'ave if this comes up.
BISHOP. Really!
WILLIE. They swear, you know.
BISHOP. So I'm told.
WILLIE. Ar! My auntie 'as one—called 'er an old cow the other day.

(PENELOPE *rises, fearing for a moment that this is "it", that the Bishop must hit the ceiling now*)

PENELOPE (*moving to* L *of the sofa*) Willie, will you explain to the Bishop what you would be very grateful if he would do?
WILLIE (*solidly*) Ar!

(*The* BISHOP *looks at Willie for the briefest moment*)

IDA (*leaning across the Bishop to Willie*) Well, *get* on.
WILLIE. Ar! (*He takes the paper from the Bishop*) 'Scuse me.

(WILLIE, *like* IDA, *is not now in awe of the Bishop, but his attitude to him is never rude or aggressive*)

(*He finds the place in the paper. To the Bishop*) Well, it's to do with football, see?
BISHOP. Football?
WILLIE. You 'eard of it?
BISHOP. A fine manly game. (*He looks at Willie*) You should play it, my boy; do you good.
WILLIE (*protesting*) I *do* play it.
BISHOP. You do? (*He looks at Willie. Quietly*) Then perhaps you should give it up.
WILLIE. I play in goal—when it's fine.
BISHOP (*blinking*) And—er—when it's wet?
WILLIE. Then I don't play.
BISHOP. No?
WILLIE. I let Mr Toop play instead.
BISHOP (*murmuring*) Good heavens!

WILLIE (*with a laugh*) I'm not daft.
BISHOP (*solemnly*) I see; you're *not*—he *is*.
WILLIE. He's not very good.
PENELOPE. Willie!
WILLIE. He looks all right. You ought to see 'im.
BISHOP (*to Penelope; with meaning*) I should *like* to see him—very much.
PENELOPE (*lamely*) He—he isn't playing today.
BISHOP (*with a glance towards the cupboard*) Not *football*, he isn't. (*Firmly*) I should like a word with him—when he has finished his—er—devotions. (*To Willie*) What exactly . . . ?
WILLIE (*pointing to the paper*) Well, you see all them names?

(*The* BISHOP *nods*)

And the figures next to 'em? Well, the names are the teams, see?
BISHOP. I see.
WILLIE. And the figures are the scores, see?

(*The* BISHOP *nods*)

Well, I'm going to read out the names, and I want you to read out the figures after 'em. (*He looks at the Bishop*) Think you can manage?
BISHOP. I shall do my best.
IDA. That's what I like to see—a willing 'orse.

(*The* BISHOP *reacts*)

WILLIE (*handing the paper to the Bishop*) Right, then. Ready? (*He spreads his coupon on his knees and reads*) "Arsenal—*Wolves*."
BISHOP (*looking at the paper*) Arsenal—Wolves. Wo—(*He looks at Willie. Faintly incredulous*) *Wolves?*
WILLIE. Ar! (*He looks at the Bishop*) Oh, no. (*He laughs, not too loudly, for quite a time*)

(*The* BISHOP *waits patiently for Willie's laughter to subside*)

They're not *really* wolves.
BISHOP (*quietly*) No?
WILLIE (*after another long, indulgent laugh*) *No!* They're *Wolverhampton Wanderers*. "Wolves" is just short, see?
BISHOP (*quietly*) I think so. These wolves are *not* wolves, just *wanderers* from *Wolverhampton*.
WILLIE (*with the very slightest impatience*) Well, what's the *result?*
BISHOP (*quietly*) I should say—offhand—a *very* lucky escape.
WILLIE (*pointing to the paper*) I mean the figures.
BISHOP. Oh—the *figures*—er—yes. (*He consults the paper*) Ah, yes. (*He reads very deliberately*) "Arsenal—*two*—er—Wolves—*two*."
IDA, WILLIE (*together*) Yes! Yes!
PENELOPE. Have we won?
WILLIE (*excitedly*) You see! I *knew* I was right.
IDA (*to the Bishop*) Oh, Your Grace, aren't you clever! But then, of course—you're *educated*.

(*The* BISHOP *blinks at Ida*)

BISHOP. I'm glad I was able to oblige. (*He rises*)
WILLIE (*putting his hand on the Bishop's arm to stop him; excitedly*) 'Alf a minute, chum.

(*The* BISHOP *looks at Willie*)

(*He corrects himself*) Your 'Ighness. We 'aven't finished yet.
BISHOP. Not?
WILLIE. Oo! Not by a long chalk. (*He draws the Bishop down on to the sofa. Kindly*) You sit down again.
BISHOP. But I want to have a word with Mr Toop.
WILLIE. We've got seven more results yet.
BISHOP. Seven?
WILLIE. And we want them all to be draws.
BISHOP. Draws?
WILLIE. Ar, 'cos you get three points for a draw.
BISHOP. I'll accept your word for it.
WILLIE. And eight threes is twenty-four, isn't it?
BISHOP. Eight twos are sixteen—eight threes are . . . Quite correct.
WILLIE. And twenty-four's the 'ighest number of points you can get. And that's what I think we've got. Now, where were we? Chelsea—Sheffield Wednesday.

(IDA *unconsciously slips her arm around the Bishop's shoulders. The* BISHOP *reacts.* IDA *removes her arm*)

BISHOP (*reading*) "Chelsea—four; Sheffield Wednesday—four."
WILLIE (*excitedly*) Yes! Yes! (*To Penelope*) That's another draw, Mrs Toop.
IDA (*indicating the Bishop*) Oo'm! Isn't he the cat's whiskers?
PENELOPE (*distrait*) You're the cat's whiskers, Uncle, but don't lose your head.
BISHOP. *You* appear to have lost your husband.
WILLIE. Now. (*He refers to his coupon*) Luton—Liverpool.
BISHOP (*searching*) Luton—Liverpool? (*Quickly*) "Luton—O . . . (*He pronounces it "oh"*)
WILLIE (*explaining*) Not "oh"—"ort"—for nil.
BISHOP. "Luton—ort—nought; Liverpool—nought."
WILLIE }
IDA } (*together*) Yes.
WILLIE. That's—(*quickly*) one, two, three. (*To the Bishop*) You feeling all right?
BISHOP. Quite, thank you. And you?
WILLIE. Ar, proper. (*He refers to the coupon*) Cardiff—Preston North End?
BISHOP (*reading*) "Cardiff—one; Preston North End—one."
WILLIE }
IDA } (*together*) Yes! Yes!
LIONEL (*in the cupboard; loudly*) No! No!

(*The* BISHOP, WILLIE *and* IDA *start and look out front.* PENELOPE *freezes, then the others turn and look at her*)

PENELOPE (*limply*) I didn't say anything.
BISHOP (*to Willie*) Er—shall we press on?

(WILLIE, *slightly subdued by shock, refers to the coupon*)

WILLIE. Brighton and 'Ove Albion—Norwich?
BISHOP (*murmuring*) Norwich. *Charming* city; and the cathedral—indescribably beautiful.
PENELOPE (*crossing above the sofa to the fireplace*) Uncle, get on.

(*The* BISHOP, *for a moment is lost in thought. The others sit quite still. At last he becomes aware of the silence, clears his throat and concentrates on the newspaper*)

BISHOP. Ahem! Er—Bognor Regis *what* did you say?
WILLIE (*not offensively*) Brighton and 'Ove *Albion.*
BISHOP. Ah, the *Albion* at Brighton—a lovely hotel.
PENELOPE. Never mind the *Albion Hotel.*
BISHOP (*without confusion*) I *beg* your pardon. (*He refers to the paper*) "Brighton and Hove Albion—two; Norwich—*two.*"
WILLIE
PENELOPE } (*together*) *Yes! Yes!*
IDA
PENELOPE (*breaking the tension; excitedly*) How many more are there, Willie? (*She sits on the desk stool*)
WILLIE (*excitedly*) Three'm.
IDA. Oo! Isn't it *exciting!*

(IDA, *still on her knees on the sofa, jogs up and down in her excitement, causing the* BISHOP *to do likewise. After bearing with this for a moment or two, the* BISHOP *slowly turns his blank gaze on Ida.* IDA, *still jogging, smiles at him, then it dawns on her that, perhaps . . . She stops jogging*)

I'm sorry.
BISHOP. Not at all.
IDA. But you should have said . . .
BISHOP (*after a pregnant pause*) Next, please.
WILLIE (*referring to the coupon*) Southampton—Scunthorpe?
BISHOP (*his face expressing nothing, but his voice everything*) *Scun*thorpe! "Southampton—two; *Scun*thorpe—two."

(*There are cries of delight from* IDA *and* WILLIE)

PENELOPE (*rising*) Three cheers for Scunthorpe. Hip, hip . . .

(*The* BISHOP *looks at Penelope.* PENELOPE *subsides and resumes her seat*)

WILLIE (*excitedly*) Heart of Midlothian—Celtic?
BISHOP (*sentimentally*) Ah! Bonnie Scotland!
PENELOPE. Och aye! (*She rises, sings and dances across to the armchair*) "The Campbells are coming . . ." Sorry. (*She sits in the armchair*)

BISHOP (*reading*) "Heart of Midlothian—four; Celtic—four."
WILLIE } (*together*) Yes! Yes!
IDA }
WILLIE. Now the last one.
IDA. The *last one*. Ooo! I can't *bear* it. (*To the Bishop*) Can you?
BISHOP (*quietly*) I shall make the attempt.
WILLIE (*his voice almost a croak*) Hibernian—Motherwell?
BISHOP (*searching; murmuring*) Hibernian—Motherwell.
IDA. Oh, dear! (*She taps the Bishop on the shoulder*) Look! You don't want me to scream, do you?
BISHOP (*quietly*) I'd rather you didn't. (*He finds the place. With no emotion whatsoever*) "Hibernian—*nought*; Motherwell . . ."

(MISS SKILLON *bursts in from the hall*)

MISS SKILLON (*as she enters; triumphantly*) *Now*, Mrs Toop, I wonder what you will have to say!

(PENELOPE, IDA *and* WILLIE *give little startled gasps and cries as Miss Skillon's voice breaks in on their intense concentration. The* BISHOP *merely lowers the paper and looks up*)

(*She crosses to* C) A man—stark naked—has been seen running over Middlewick Moor.
PENELOPE. *What?*
MISS SKILLON. From details given, I have reasons to believe that man is Mr Toop.
PENELOPE (*after the slightest pause; coldly*) I shall not ask what those details are. (*She laughs, then checks herself*)
IDA (*to the Bishop*) Oh—do go on, sir.
WILLIE (*taking the paper from the Bishop*) 'Ere, let me 'ave it.
MISS SKILLON (*crossing and snatching the paper from Willie*) This is no time to be reading newspapers.

(WILLIE *and* IDA *protest*)

(*She crosses to* C) Mrs Toop, didn't you hear me say the man is running about *stark naked?*
PENELOPE. Well, if that's the way he *likes* to run about . . .
MISS SKILLON. Mrs Toop, are you devoid of feeling for your husband altogether? I insist that you take your car and identify . . .
PENELOPE (*rising; very firmly*) Miss Skillon, I draw the line at playing hide and seek with naked men on Middlewick Moor.
MISS SKILLON (*fuming*) Very well. I shall go myself. *I* have no qualms.
PENELOPE (*moving to* L *of the armchair; muttering*) I'll bet you haven't.
MISS SKILLON (*barking*) Briggs!
WILLIE (*rising*) Sir—er . . .
MISS SKILLON. You can drive, can't you?
WILLIE. Yes, but we . . .
MISS SKILLON. You will get the Vicar's car out of the garage at once and drive me to Middlewick Moor.

WILLIE. But, Miss Skillon . . .
MISS SKILLON (*overriding*) No time must be lost. There's an east wind blowing.

(IDA *rises. She and* WILLIE *move up* C)

Mrs Toop, will you please get me something to drape over your husband.
PENELOPE (*beginning to really lose her temper*) Miss Skillon, if you would only . . .
MISS SKILLON. Very well, I shall help myself. (*She crosses to the cupboard, opens the door and gives a cry of alarm on seeing Lionel and Humphrey inside*)

(IDA *and* WILLIE *react with cries of surprise. The* BISHOP *sits on the sofa, "aware" but completely "dead-pan"*)

(*Unable to believe her eyes*) Mr *Toop!* Why aren't you stark naked on Middlewick Moor?

(LIONEL *gapes at Miss Skillon*)

LIONEL (*in an agonized bleat*) Penelope! She's gone mad. (*He comes from the cupboard and goes down* LC)
PENELOPE (*moving towards Lionel*) Lionel, darling . . .

(HUMPHREY, *newspaper in hand, emerges from the cupboard and crosses above the sofa to* R)

(*With surprise*) And Mr Humphrey. (*She crosses to* L *of Humphrey*) So *that's* where you were. You know—we missed you.
HUMPHREY (*very wretchedly*) Mrs Toop . . .

(MISS SKILLON *closes the cupboard door and stands above the left end of the sofa*)

PENELOPE (*automatically smoothing out the front of his surplice*) Now, what could you possibly have been doing in that cupboard?
HUMPHREY. Mrs Toop . . .
PENELOPE (*turning Humphrey round and smoothing the back of his surplice*) Good heavens, Mr Humphrey, you don't have to explain. (*She gives the surplice a final tug and turns him to face her*) After all—(*she crosses to* R *of Lionel*) boys will be boys. (*She tidies Lionel's hair*) Just *what were* you up to?
LIONEL. Penelope. I . . . (*He waves his hand with the coupon in it despairingly*)
PENELOPE (*her eyes lighting on the coupon*) What have you got there? (*She snatches the coupon and gapes at it*) A Pools coupon. (*She gapes at Lionel*) So *that's* what you were both . . . Lionel! *You* doing Football Pools. You! After all your lecturing about gambling—there you were, in the cupboard, doing out a—a Pool with Mr Humphrey. (*With false disapproval*) And *Mr* Humphrey!
HUMPHREY (*desperately and hurriedly*) I had to try *something*, Mrs Toop. My death-watch beetle—my motor scooter . . .
LIONEL (*in a croaking voice*) My new bells!

(*The* Bishop *picks up the "Church Times" from the sofa seat*)

Penelope (*sympathetically*) Oh, you poor darlings—so that's why . . . (*To Humphrey*) You wanted a "death-watch beetle" and a "scooter"—and you—(*she turns to Lionel*) wanted new church bells.

Miss Skillon. And what about my bicycle?

Penelope. Well—darlings—there is *just* a chance that . . .

(*The front-door bell rings*)

Now, there's someone at the front door. Don't you bother, Uncle, I'll go.

(Penelope *exits to the hall*)

Willie (*moving above the sofa; to the Bishop*) Go on, sir! Read it! Read it!

Bishop (*reading from the "Church Times"*) "The Dean of St Paul's addressing the Anti-Gambling League . . ."

(Willie *snatches the newspaper from Miss Skillon and hands it to the Bishop*)

Willie. No, no, not that one—this one. We've got seven right.

Ida. And there's only one more to read.

Lionel (*moving* c) What's this? The Bishop doing Pools? Can I believe my ears?

Bishop (*looking at Lionel's attire*) Can I believe my *eyes?*

(Lionel *tries to cover his gum-boots with his surplice*)

Willie. Go on, sir. Hibernian—Motherwell.

Bishop (*reading*) "Hibernian—two; Motherwell—two."

Ida, Willie (*together*) We've won!

(*The others react.*
Penelope, *wild-eyed and gibbering, rushes in from the hall*)

Penelope (*as she enters; wildly*) Lionel! Lionel!

Lionel (*moving to Penelope; anxiously*) What is it?

Penelope (*pointing off* l) He—he's on the doorstep.

Lionel (*crossing to the arch*) I'll remove him at once. (*He stops and turns*) *Who* is?

Penelope. His car's broken down in the village.

Lionel. *Whose has?*

Penelope. He wants some lunch.

Lionel (*almost shouting*) Who does?

Willie. Mr Cope?

Penelope. No. The—the Archbishop of Canterbury.

Lionel *and* Humphrey *give yelps of horror.*
Humphrey *dashes out of the french windows.* Lionel, *after a quick look of horror at his attire, moves to the cupboard as—*

the Curtain *falls*

The CURTAIN *rises as quickly as possible on a clear stage for "calls". The calls are actually the climax of the Play, as it makes it quite clear to the audience that Penelope and Company have won a large sum of money. The calls are taken singly.*

WILLIE *enters from the kitchen, carrying a huge parrot-cage with a parrot in it.*

MISS SKILLON *enters by the french windows wheeling a brand new bicycle.*

HUMPHREY *emerges from the cupboard wearing a crash helmet and a pair of goggles under his chin.*

IDA *enters from the kitchen, wearing a fur coat and carrying another over her arm. She wears a small diamond tiara.*

The BISHOP *enters by the french windows, wearing a shining new bishop's tophat.*

LIONEL *enters down the stairs. As he does so a wonderful peal of church bells crashes out and gradually increases in volume throughout the remainder of the calls.* LIONEL *goes to the french windows for a moment, looks off in the direction of the bells, then, with a happy smile on his face, takes his position for the call.*

PENELOPE *enters from the kitchen, pushing a shopping basket on wheels, filled with the largest possible size tins of corned beef.*

When they are finally in position, with the bells at the top of their crescendo—

the CURTAIN *falls*

FURNITURE AND PROPERTY LIST

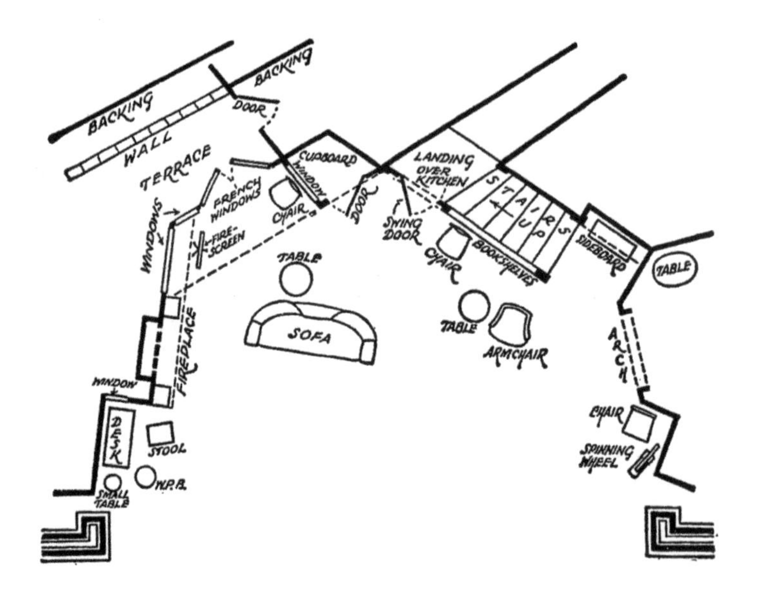

ACT I

On stage: Small table (down R) *On it:* pipe stand-cum-tobacco jar with 6 pipes

Waste-paper basket (full)

Desk. *On top shelf:* challenge cup, 3 Christmas cards, brass lamp

On second shelf: 2 painted wooden candlesticks, brown glass cigarette box, Christmas card

On flap: blotter and flat blotter, wooden letter-rack, pens, pencils, notepaper, ashtray, envelopes

In pigeon-holes: exercise-book, copy of *Lady Chatterley's Lover*, dressing

Desk stool

Bellows (hanging below fireplace)

Shovel, poker, tongs (hanging above fireplace)

In fireplace: copper kettle, black china cat

On mantelpiece: box with cigarettes, matches, lighter, clock, gong, pair brass candlesticks, pair vases with spills, pair bronze vases

On extension: radio, brass lamp

Warming-pan (hanging above upstage end of mantelpiece) *In it:* sixpence

Over mantelpiece: 3 hunting horns with holly
Window curtains and pelmet
Tapestry firescreen (up R)
Sofa. *On it:* cushions, library book
Table (behind sofa) *On it:* telephone, pad and pencil, ashtray
Upright chair (up C)
Upright chair (L) *On it:* book
Armchair (LC) *On it:* cushion
Table (LC) *On it:* magazines, copies of *Punch* and *Church Times*, ashtray, tobacco jar
On floor down R *of table* LC: tobacco
Built-in bookshelves. *On top shelf:* ornaments, Christmas cards
In shelves: books
Sideboard. *In it:* elderberry wine, 2 glasses
In drawer: dressing
Stair carpet
On landing rail: holly
On wall L: wall-bracket with holly
At top of stairs: light switches
Over arch: holly
Above arch: light switches
On wall above sideboard: 2 mirrors, religious plaque with holly
Carved oak chair (down L)
Spinning-wheel (down L)
On wall down L: wooden elephant head with vase of holly
Carpet (R)
Carpet (L)
Rug (down C)
On wall above kitchen door: 3 pictures
In cupboard: practical light and switch, umbrellas, sticks, large surplice, laundry basket, gum-boots, plastic mackintosh, scarf
In hall backing: oval table. *On it:* vase with white roses
On hall backing: barometer, wall-bracket light with holly

Windows closed
Window curtains closed
Doors closed
Fire on
All light fittings on

Off stage: Tray. *On it:* cup of coffee, bowl of sugar (IDA)

Personal: IDA: handbag. *In it:* compact
LIONEL: handkerchief, pipe
MISS SKILLON: handbag
WILLIE: Cope's pool coupon

ACT II

Strike: All ornaments, etc., from floor R
Pools coupon
Book from sofa
Tobacco jar from table LC
Replace chair L

Set: *In front of fireplace:* dustpan, brush, Christmas cards and spills from mantelpiece, broken china
On left end of sofa: duster
On mantelpiece: nude statue, lying flat
On upstage edge of desk: pencil
On table LC: lighter
Windows closed
Window curtains open
Doors closed
Fire on
Light fittings off

Off stage: Tray. *On it:* ornaments, clock (PENELOPE)
Stick (LIONEL)
Medical bag. *In it:* rubber gloves, stethoscope (MISS SKILLON)
Bowl and towel (IDA)
Sunday paper (WILLIE)
Mixing bowl and spoon (PENELOPE)
Small bag (HUMPHREY)
Tartan travelling rug (LIONEL)

Personal: WILLIE: bag of humbugs, art magazine
HUMPHREY: Pools coupon

ACT III

Strike: Dustpan and brush
Bowl and towel
Bowl and spoon

Set: Willie's Pools coupon under edge of carpet
Red Cross tin and flags on floor below armchair
Book on mantelpiece
Tidy room generally
French windows open
Doors closed
Fire on
Light fittings off

Off stage: Ordnance map (Miss Skillon)
Telescope (Miss Skillon)
Tray. *On it:* cup of coffee (Penelope)
Tin of corned beef (Ida)
Copy of the *News of the World* (Ida)
Bag (Bishop)
Coat (Bishop)
Homburg hat with rosette (Bishop)
Old bicycle (Miss Skillon)
Humphrey's Pools coupon (Willie)
Parrot in cage (Willie)
New bicycle (Miss Skillon)
Crash helmet, goggles (Humphrey)
2 fur coats, tiara (Ida)
Tophat (Bishop)
Shopping basket on wheels. *In it:* large tins of corned beef (Penelope)

Personal: Humphrey: handkerchief
Penelope: wrist watch
Willie: newspaper

LIGHTING PLOT

Property fittings required: fire-grate, 5-branch chandelier, 2 pairs wall-brackets, 2 table-lamps, practical light and switch in cupboard up L

Interior. A lounge-hall. The same scene throughout

THE MAIN ACTING AREAS are down R, at a sofa RC, C, up L, and at an armchair LC

THE APPARENT SOURCES OF LIGHT are, in daytime, french windows up RC, and small windows down R, up R and at the top of the stairs up L; and at night, a 5-branched chandelier C, table-lamps down R and up R and wall-brackets L and in the hall backing down L

ACT I. Evening

To open: All light fittings on, except bracket in hall backing
Fire on
Cupboard light off
Blue outside windows
Flood in hall backing down L, off
Flood in door backing up L, on
Flood at head of stairs, off

Cue 1 IDA switches off lights (Page 2)
Black-Out

Cue 2 IDA switches on chandelier (Page 2)
Snap in chandelier
Snap in covering lights

Cue 3 IDA: "... or goin', do 'e?" (Page 4)
Snap on bracket and flood in backing down L

Cue 4 LIONEL switches out hall light (Page 4)
Snap out bracket and flood in backing down L

Cue 5 LIONEL switches off chandelier (Page 4)
Black-Out

Cue 6 LIONEL switches on chandelier (Page 4)
Snap in chandelier
Snap in covering lights

Cue 7 IDA switches out chandelier (Page 5)
Black-Out

Cue 8 IDA switches on chandelier (Page 5)
Snap in chandelier
Snap in covering lights

Cue 9 IDA switches on hall light (Page 13)
Snap on bracket and flood in backing down L

ACT II. Morning

To open: All light fittings off
Effect of winter daylight
Fire on
Cupboard light off
Flood in hall backing down L, on
Flood in door backing up L, on
Flood at head of stairs, on

No cues

ACT III. Morning

To open: Lights as at the end of the previous Act

No cues

EFFECTS PLOT

ACT I

Cue 1	At rise of CURTAIN *Telephone gives long rings*	(Page 1,
Cue 2	IDA: "... walls have ears." *Sound of car horn and car arriving and stopping*	(Page 3)
Cue 3	PENELOPE: "... health than temper." *Front-door bell rings off* L	(Page 13)
Cue 4	PENELOPE switches on radio ANNOUNCER'S *voice through radio*	(Page 13)
Cue 5	PENELOPE switches on radio *"The Ride of the Valkyries" at full volume*	(Page 13)
Cue 6	PENELOPE hits radio *Stop music abruptly*	(Page 14)

ACT II

Cue 7	PENELOPE: "... been through all ..." *Front-door bell rings*	(Page 35)
Cue 8	HUMPHREY sits on sofa *Crash in kitchen*	(Page 41)
Cue 9	IDA: "... we waiting for?" *2 very cracked church bells ring*	(Page 47)
Cue 10	HUMPHREY exits by the french windows *Telephone rings*	(Page 48)
Cue 11	PENELOPE: "Oh, no!" *Stop church bells*	(Page 48)

ACT III

Cue 12	HUMPHREY: "Ah! There it is." *Front-door bell rings*	(Page 59)
Cue 13	PENELOPE: "... a chance that ..." *Front-door bell rings*	(Page 74)
Cue 14	LIONEL enters down the stairs *Peal of church bells*	(Page 75)

Lightning Source UK Ltd.
Milton Keynes UK
UKHW021457150319
339224UK00005B/223/P